JUN 31 '82

2

W9-DCP-152

The Rape of Art

We are barbarians and we wish to be
barbarians. It is an honourable calling

ADOLF HITLER

THE
RAPE OF ART

The Story of Hitler's Plunder
of the Great Masterpieces of Europe

BY
DAVID ROXAN and KEN WANSTALL

COWARD-McCANN, Inc.
New York

Contents

Illustrations

ILLUSTRATIONS

Hradčany Castle, Prague, where Hitler spent his first night on Czechoslovakian soil, 15 March 1938. He left next morning with a number of stolen tapestries*

The glorious Veit Stoss altar from the Church of St Mary in Cracow. Commissioned by the King of Poland and carved between 1477 and 1487, it was confiscated by the Nazis because Veit Stoss was a German from Nuremberg*

Governor-General Hans Frank greets his guests at a Nazi reception in Cracow. Under his rule, Poland was picked clean of her art treasures within six months*

Breughel's 'The Hay Harvest', part of the Lobkowitz collection in Prague, seized by Dr Posse and entered as Item 2124 in the Linz archives (*National Gallery, Prague*)

Detail from the famous Hohenfurth altarpiece from Czechoslovakia confiscated by the Nazis in April 1941 and subsequently seized by Hitler for his Linz collection*

The Castle Square, Warsaw, with the Royal Castle, which was ruthlessly looted by the Nazis and most of its interior decorations badly damaged (*Joseph Ellner*)

Castle Square on Liberation Day—17 January 1945. The Polish flag flies proudly from the pedestal of the destroyed monument to King Sigismund III (*Keystone Press*)

The moment of looting. In France a masterpiece by Tintoretto is inspected by a Nazi officer before shipment to Germany, where Hitler always had first choice of the spoils (*Keystone Press*)

Martin Bormann, who quickly realized how important Linz was to his Fuehrer, and devoted himself to administering its every detail

Following page 116

Alfred Rosenberg, director of the main Nazi looting organization in Paris who sided with Goering in his rivalry with Hitler to obtain the great masterpieces. He was hanged at Nuremberg as a war criminal (*Camera Press*)

Michelangelo's masterpiece, the Madonna and Child, was looted by the Germans from the Church of Notre-Dame in Bruges and transported across Europe*

'The Last Supper', painted by the fifteenth-century Netherlands painter, Dirk Bouts, for the Church of St Peter at Louvain; hidden at Alt Aussee (*Mansell Collection*)

Botticelli's 'Simonetta', purchased by Hitler in 1938 for 300,000 reichsmarks from the dealer Walter Bornheim after a plot claiming that it was irreparably damaged

A bust of Karl Haberstock, the German art dealer who made a fortune out of selling Hitler pictures for his Linz collection*

Dr Hermann Voss, Director of the Wiesbaden Gallery, who succeeded Dr Posse as head of the Sonderauftrag Linz, though with considerably reduced powers*

ILLUSTRATIONS

The Van Eyck brothers' 'Adoration of the Lamb', painted in 1432 for the Cathedral of St Bavon at Ghent: hidden at Alt Aussee (*Mansell Collection*)

Schloss Weesenstein, near Dresden, where Hitler stored large numbers of prints and drawings. The building was taken by the Russians in 1945*

The Meyer Madonna by Holbein, part of the Schloss Museum collection at Darmstadt, one of the few masterpieces admired by Hitler which he was never able to obtain (*Mansell Collection*)

Hermann Goering and Prince Philipp von Hessen, who became the main Linz agent in Italy, buying numerous paintings for Hitler. He was a descendant of Emperor Frederick III of Prussia and Queen Victoria*

Paintings from Monte Cassino arriving at the Vatican for safe-keeping under the direction of the Germans after the collapse of Italy. Many others were looted en route

The creation of Mad Ludwig of Bavaria, Schloss Neuschwanstein became a vast treasure-house when it was chosen as the main repository of the Einsatzstab Rosenberg (*Foto Arnold*)

A miscellaneous collection of art treasures in a typical storeroom in the Schloss Neuschwanstein†

Bad Aussee in the Austrian Alps, some seventy miles south-east of Salzburg and only a few miles from the Alt Aussee salt-mine*

The administration buildings of the Alt Aussee salt-mine taken over by the Nazis as the final main repository for Hitler's vast Linz collection†

Panels of the Ghent altarpiece stored underground at Alt Aussee. On the left is the art restorer Karl Sieber, who did more than anyone to prevent the mine being blown up†

One of the large chambers in the Alt Aussee salt-mine, divided by stout storage racks. In the foreground a hygrometer to check the humidity of the air†

The 'Madonna and Child' being carefully hauled out of the Alt Aussee salt-mine by uniformed American art experts. It was restored to Bruges in September 1947†

The slow process of reparation. Recovered art treasures were stored in racks at the Central Collecting Point in Munich before their rightful owners were discovered†

Heinrich Hoffmann, Hitler's official photographer, after his capture by the Allies in 1945 (*Copress, Munich*)

* *Ullstein Verlag, Berlin.*
† *From the collection of Mr Thomas Carr Howe, Jnr.*

Preface

The growth of the Nazi empire before and during the Second World War saw the looting of art treasures on a scale unprecedented in European history. As each helpless country fell before the invader so were its national treasures, and many world-famous collections belonging to private citizens, swallowed up, taken into 'protective custody' by the Nazi machine, and all trace of them was lost.

Soon after the D-Day invasion of Hitler's Europe, art and museum experts in uniform followed the advancing Allied armies with the sole purpose of tracking down looted art treasures and returning them to their rightful owners, following clues that were often no more than rumours and unravelling a tangled sequence of events. Their work was given high priority for General Eisenhower fully recognized the importance of making speedy reparations, particularly of national art treasures, if he was not to lose the goodwill of the liberated countries.

These experts in uniform formed the Art Looting Investigation Unit of the U.S. Office of Strategic Services. They were recruited, commissioned and trained in America. They were super-detectives, carrying out a task unique in history. At the end of their labours they produced three major reports, dealing with the Hitler collection, the Goering collection and the Einsatzstab Rosenberg, the official Nazi looting organization. They also wrote a number of minor reports.

Distribution of these reports was severely restricted. Each was marked 'Confidential' and less than fifty copies were issued to various military and civil bodies. These included the United States Chief of Counsel at Nuremberg; the United States Group C.C. (Germany); the Theatre JA War Crimes Branch at Frankfurt; the British Control Commission; the Roberts commission; the G.5 Civil Affairs of the U.S. War Department; M.I.5. and M.I.6; and the Economic Warfare Department of the U.S. State Department.

Nearly twenty years later all these reports still remain unpublished, nor is there any intention that they should be published. They are held by the National Archives and Records Service in Washington, which considers them to be controversial, and they remain the hidden property of the State Department.

By a fortuitous chain of circumstances, one of these reports fell into our hands. Known as Consolidated Interrogation Report No. 4, it is a bulky document that tells of the personal looting carried out by Hitler himself and his plans to transform his home-town of Linz in Austria into the cultural Mecca of the New Europe. This document forms the basis of our book, revealing a piece of untold history of the Second World War and throwing new light on the character of the Fuehrer.

Faced with the *fait accompli* of the report being in our hands, the Director of the World War II Records Division of the National Archives and Records Service in Washington agreed to the removal of its security classification, but our application to see other minor interrogation reports pertinent to it was refused. These include those we know were written after the interrogation of such principals as Hermann Voss, Karl Haberstock and Heinrich Hoffmann.

Whatever the reasons for claiming that these reports must still be classified as 'restricted' at this distance from the Second World War, the decision can only arouse the worst kind of speculation.

D.R. and K.W.

Notes

All quotations in the text are taken from the translations of the Consolidated Interrogation Report mentioned above. These translations were made by U.S. Army officers, who worked under heavy pressure at the time of the original investigation.

All sums of money are given in reichsmarks. The value of a pre-war reichsmark was approximately twice that of the present-day deutschmark.

Acknowledgement

The authors would like to thank Mr Thomas Carr Howe, Jnr., for allowing them to use material from his book *Salt Mines and Castles* (Bobbs-Merrill Co. Inc., 1946) and for supplying illustrations; and the Wiener Library for valuable help with illustration research.

CHAPTER ONE

Birth of a Dream

It was 8 p.m. in the town of Linz, dowdy provincial capital of Upper Austria. The date was 11 March 1938. In the bright evening moonlight more than a hundred thousand people— four-fifths of the entire population—were milling in the streets, shouting themselves hoarse, hysterically waving tiny Swastika flags. Larger Swastikas covered the buildings, as if this was a celebration instead of a capitulation. All eyes were fixed on the slowly driven open Mercedes-Benz. Standing in it, genuinely dazed by the adulation he was receiving, was Adolf Hitler. The small boy had made good and was returning to his home-town to face a delirious welcome. It was a traumatic experience from which a great deal was to come.

Hitler had ordered his troops into Austria without any clear plan of what he would do next. He was playing it by ear, as he had done so before and was to do so again, probing to discover how much he could get away with. He himself had crossed the border at his birthplace of Braunau-am-Inn with some vague idea of a negotiated settlement with the Austrian Government in Vienna, leaving himself room to manœuvre a retreat if the opposition from the rest of Europe became too great. He had not even considered an Anschluss, which was to be handed to him less than a month later by 99.7% of the people when Austria voted.

But that was in the future. On this March evening in Linz he was facing his first personal reception in a foreign town of any size. It was rapturous, overwhelming, and was to have a decisive effect on his megalomania. As the crowds cheered like demented beings, the Mercedes made its way yard by yard to the Town Hall. As with any practised politician, Hitler was adept at producing tears of emotion but this time there was reason to believe they were genuine. He addressed the worshipping townspeople from the balcony, recalling the time when he had left Linz almost as an outcast. He went on: 'I have believed in my task, I have lived for it and I have fought for it, and you are all my witnesses that I have accomplished it, my witnesses and my guarantors.' These words sent the crowds into an even greater frenzy. It was some time before they were quiet enough for Hitler to add: 'I believe I shall be able to point with pride to my homeland before the whole German people.' But by his gesture, he meant Linz, not Austria. It was the first hint of the grandiose plan that was to be his obsession for the next and last seven years of his life.

*

By 1938 Hitler had achieved a miracle within Germany. Production was booming, unemployment a spectre of the past, but the price was high. Rearmament was being carried out at a cost so staggering that the Nazis were billions of marks in debt. More years of peace could only have disastrous economic results, yet it was not this that turned Hitler's mind towards the paths of war.

In Germany he had gained total power and was becoming drunk with it. He had shaken up the Army and Foreign Ministry, thrown away Hindenburg's political testament like so much waste-paper. More and more he was talking of 'the supreme mission of the German people'. The shrewd politician didn't want to fight the whole of Europe but forces within him turned him deaf to the pleas of moderation from the other Nazi leaders. He was starting to believe that his destiny was to create a New Europe and now Linz had rapturously received him, causing him to decide to gamble for the whole of Austria, persuading him that everywhere people were waiting for the coming of the Fuehrer. On that March night Linz pushed him firmly on to the tiger's back.

Hitler had arrived in Linz on a Saturday evening and should have left for Vienna the next morning. Instead he stayed on, visiting his parents' graves, basking in the adulation that was to be repeated after his 120-mile journey to Vienna on the Monday and again four months later at a great German sports festival in Breslau when the people of the Sudetenland marched past, crying out for the Fuehrer to liberate them. But it was the voice of Linz that had been the first voice, making him feel he was on a gambler's winning streak and that his luck would not change. It was Linz, where he had spent his youth, that had so dramatically reinforced his dreams of power. During the thirty-six hours he spent in this unimportant town the grandiose plan that had so long been in his mind at last found expression. He spoke of it first to Professor Kerschner, Director of the town's Provincial Museum, and that first utterance was like a dam breaking, the ideas pouring forth in endless succession. Ideas that would glorify his memory on a scale not even equalled by that other military dictator, Napoleon, and wipe out for evermore the failures, hatreds and humiliations of the past that still haunted him.

*

Adolf Hitler's life from birth until the First World War and Munich politics finally claimed him clearly shows strands, some real and some Hitler-invented, that plaited together were to form the rope of action during that March week-end in Linz. It was no sudden impulse that lay behind his vision but a burgeoning of seeds planted long ago in childhood and his miserable youth.

Born in 1889 at Braunau on the River Inn, the young Adolf achieved excellent results at his primary school, one teacher describing him as 'very much alert, obedient, and lively'. When he entered the secondary school in nearby Linz in 1900, he did not fulfil his early promise. His reports contained such remarks as 'below standard' and 'irregular'. His failure to justify his early promise was more due to bone-idleness than lack of intelligence. He was a bitter disappointment to his father, Alois, a retired customs officer living off his pension, who spared himself further worry about his wayward son by dying in 1903. Hitler moved with his mother, Frau Klara Hitler, to Linz so as to be nearer his school, but that did not improve his work. His disgusted teachers claimed that he was only proficient in gymnastics, being well below standard in every other subject. After his fourth year he was asked to remove himself.

The fifteen-year-old Hitler made one more attempt at schooling. He went to a secondary school at Steyr, about fifteen miles from his home, but again he got poor results though it was stated that his moral conduct was 'very satisfactory', a judgement that millions would not have agreed with in later years. After one year Hitler quit school, deciding he would be far happier at home with his mother where no one would complain of his indolence.

In the following May Hitler paid his first visit to Vienna. He stayed a fortnight, just one amongst thousands of provincial youths awed by the glittering brilliance of Emperor Francis Joseph's capital. Already a fervent Wagnerian, Hitler went to the opera, experiencing typically adolescent exultation at performances of *Tristan and Isolde* and *The Flying Dutchman*. He returned to a Linz whose dullness and narrow-mindedness he found he was hating more and more. He spent his time painting watercolours or making pencil copies of pictures. Significantly his biggest project during this period, which came to naught like everything else, was designing a new Linz, including a vast new Town Hall and building a large bridge across the Danube that would have disfigured the lovely countryside.

Contrary to some accounts, among them the fabrications included in *Mein Kampf*, Hitler was not cursed by poverty in his youth. His father's pension had been more than twice a working-man's wage and his mother was left comfortably off. Hitler was able to live the carefree life of a young gentleman of leisure,

4

always well-dressed and often carrying an ivory-handled walking-stick. He went for long walks, preferring his own company to other people's, a trait which did not make him very popular. He was sexually frigid, exhibiting little interest in girls. Between short bouts of drawing and longer bouts of idleness he suffered fits of depression, feeling that he was making no headway in life. He began to feel suffocated by Linz and its people. His eyes were on Vienna but as much as he wanted to swim in that larger pool, he knew he was a failure in one very much smaller. It was not in his nature to blame himself.

Early in 1907 Frau Klara was operated on for cancer of the breast. She recovered, went home, but was soon ill again. Not one to waste an opportunity, Hitler took advantage of his mother's condition, overcoming her weakened opposition to his plan to quit Linz for Vienna. Patience would not have served him ill as she died three months later. But Hitler could not wait: he reached Vienna in the early September, determined to seek fame as an artist. His first call was on the Academy of Fine Arts, where he applied for enrolment in classes in painting, producing a bulky portfolio of his drawings. He sat for an examination and his failure he later described in *Mein Kampf* as coming 'like a bolt from the blue'. Although it recognized that his artistic talent was small, the Academy suggested that he take up architecture as he could have the makings of a competent draughtsman. Hitler was eager to comply with this suggestion but was totally frustrated in his dreams of becoming a great master-builder because he lacked a diploma from his school in Linz. Once more, consciousness of failure in that backwater of a town cut deep into an already open wound.

Hitler would have had little difficulty in finding a job, being the son of a respectable Civil Servant, but he still clung to his artistic dreams. He had enough money to last him a year and, despite the Academy's verdict, he would show the world he was a great painter. He refused to consider accepting failure and returning to Linz, or to admit that his refusal to take up some office post was because he was incapable of the self-discipline necessary to hold it down.

He lived in a succession of lodgings, pursuing his illusory

dreams, each day drifting farther away from reality. His money dwindled fast because he seldom added to it, the buyers for his watercolours being few and far between. His health deteriorated and he would have become consumptive at an early age if the First World War hadn't broken out, giving the Army the honour of feeding and clothing him.

But that was still four years away. In 1910 Hitler was reduced to moving into the hostel for men at 27 Meldemannstrasse, a large residence for the young and almost penniless, and always overcrowded in a city whose bright flame attracted so many moths. Accommodation was granted only to those earning less than 1,500 kronen a year (then about £60), a bed cost three kronen a week, and each cubicle could only be occupied between 9 p.m. and 9 a.m. Hitler lived with illiterate labourers and common vagrants. To avoid being evicted, he was forced to obey strict rules. No standing on the beds, no consuming of spirits on the premises, no baths except during fixed hours, no games except chess, draughts and dominoes, no singing, no spitting except in the spittoons provided. These and many other regulations were a long way from the carefree life he had once strolled through with his ivory-handled walking-stick.

Hitler painted feverishly in the hostel's reading-room, mostly making copies. The results were hawked round the bars in Vienna but customers were few. When a sale was made, it was mainly due to the buyer being told the artist was sick and starving. When money was low, Hitler lived on a watery soup. His clothing was mainly rags, made up of an old-fashioned too-large overcoat thick with dirt and grease which would have been laughable if it hadn't been so filthy, stained and creaseless grey trousers, and cracked shoes rapidly disintegrating. He wore no shirt or underpants. In order to keep body and soul together he was forced to go into partnership with a Hungarian Jew named Josef Neumann, who tried to sell his pictures on a fifty-fifty basis.

As in Linz, Hitler was far from popular. He employed a bitter tongue to start heated political arguments in the hostel that usually ended in bad feelings on all sides. Attempts, which at first failed, were made to have him evicted, but later Hitler was forced to leave and he became one of the common vagrants he had despised so much. He slept in doss-houses or bedded himself down under archways. On warm and sometimes cold nights he slept in the Prater. There were occasions when he was forced to beg soup from a nunnery. His Vienna was made up of slums, filth, young prostitutes craving not money but a night's lodgings, and biting poverty. Though he could see it, he was a thousand miles from the city of Strauss, the Blue Danube, wealth, luxury and the endless pursuit of pleasure. Shut out from where he believed he rightfully belonged, Hitler hated Vienna. He felt cheated, deprived of his just inheritance, and later described these years as 'the most miserable time of my life', though he was quick to add that they had been a thorough schooling for the glorious deeds that were to follow. In 1913 Hitler quit Vienna for Munich, describing in *Mein Kampf* all his political, philosophical and racial reasons for doing so. His real purpose was an attempt to evade being conscripted for military service.

In the ensuing years the scars, both the real and those imagined by his twisted ego, remained with the man: his sense of failure as a boy in Linz, knowing that his image in his hometown had been denigrated and passionately wanting redress; his hatred of Vienna, wanting to humiliate it as he had been humiliated while living in it for more than five years; his total frustration because he had not fulfilled himself either as artist or architect.

The last was to remain strongly with him during the years of his rise to power. After the big Nazi rallies at Nuremberg in 1927 and 1929, Hitler ordered the building of a vast arena, sketching the first plans himself and leaving the architects to fill in the details. At Nuremberg he planned the linking of the old city to the steel and concrete towers of the Third Reich by a gigantic concrete highway over the Nuremberg ponds. His passion for architecture was so great that his aides learned always to have compasses and other drawing instruments ready in case the Fuehrer was seized by the sudden impulse to draw vast buildings, arches, theatres amd museums. Like all megalomaniacs, he wanted to change the world. Architects could change a city's skyline but he believed he could change a country's, even a continent's. He saw himself as the master-builder of the New Europe.

He no longer had time for painting but he could impose his personal vision on the world. He was the Fuehrer, able to dictate that people only enjoyed what he enjoyed. He disliked the French Impressionists so they would be totally banned. Art would be regulated by decree, the inward vision of beauty trampled on. His own appreciation did not extend beyond the chocolate-box level and the more photographic a painting was, the greater he liked it. He was prepared to accept the great masters of the past because not even he could reverse the judgement of centuries but he condemned modern art. He was insensitive, he inspired no artist of true merit in Nazi Germany. He shut out greatness because he could not understand it.

Out of this madness came the Munich Art Exhibition of 1937 the paintings for which were chosen by a committee, with Hitler having the final word. He spent hours touring the galleries, accepting or rejecting by a word. There was no appeal for his judgements were infallible and not to be questioned. He based his taste on nationalism and racialism. Great art sprang from Nordic-German roots alone and no other was acceptable.

This was the man who had received the adulation of Linz. Some historians have stated that the wild acclaim given to him on that March evening contributed as much to the Second World War as any other single event. Two days later he had strutted and preened himself in Vienna, knowing he was master of a city in which he had once starved. But the wounds of the past were too deep to be healed so quickly. And there were others still gaping wide.

*

He talked at great length to Professor Kerschner, using him as a sounding-board rather than seeking his opinions. He planned to transform Linz into the artistic Mecca of the New Europe that National Socialism was dedicated to create. This dowdy provincial capital would be rebuilt into a modern metropolis with a population three or four times as great. It would be a revolution in town planning that would dazzle all eyes. The shining heart of this great new city would be a massive array of public buildings, erected to the memory of Adolf Hitler, arch-dictator, designed by Adolf Hitler, master-builder, and filled by Adolf Hitler with the artistic treasures he would loot from the four corners of Europe.

Hitler described how the buildings would form an imposing square, each related to the next. The biggest would be the Fuehrermuseum, containing an art collection greater than any in the world. Armour would be housed in another building. More than a quarter of a million rare books and manuscripts would be in the library to glorify a man who as a boy in Linz could not spell and whose punctuation was atrocious. There would be a separate museum for sculpture, others for furniture, tapestries, rare coins and *objets d'art*. Finally, the pattern would be completed by building a large theatre. In comparison, Napoleon's Tomb in Paris would be reduced to insignificance.

Though he was interested only in the sweep of his plans and not the details, Hitler was determined personally to supervise their carrying-out. He planned a special Office of Building in Linz under his own personal direction. And no matter if he were for months on end in Berlin or wherever his solemn duties took him, everything would be submitted to him for his per-sonal approval.

The glorification of his memory in the town where he grew up was not his only aim. As Linz grew, so Vienna would be reduced. As Europe's great works of art poured into Linz, so Vienna would be stripped and starved, relegated to living only on its past glories in the New Europe ruled by the Nazis. For Hitler, the greatest balm to old wounds would be making Linz the new Vienna and Vienna just another Linz.

The gulf between Hitler's humdrum boyhood and the demoniacal genius of later years with power of life and death over millions is wide. In between there are blank pages, a lack of reasons why this one man, born as he was and in such an en-vironment, should have turned the world so terribly upside down. Yet if there is blankness in between, there are still some similarities between the young Hitler in Linz and Vienna and the aloof Fuehrer shut away in his mountain fortress, a madman running a war. Both lived within themselves, shunned human contact and indulged in fantasies. The glorification of Linz crossed the gulf between the boy and the man, bridging the hidden places which might explain so much if they could be fully uncovered.

The Linz project also had another importance beyond its own physical boundaries. It was one of the very few things in Hitler's life for which he showed any emotion. Essentially he was a cold man, incapable of loving. He had little feeling for women, the moods of Nature, friends, the family circle, his comrades-in-arms. As for Germany, he was ready to pull her down with him when his own defeat had become inevitable. But the idea of Linz stayed with him, was clung to tenaciously for seven years when so many others were forgotten. For Hitler its importance far transcended a number of buildings and what would be shown inside them, although it is an interesting fact that when Hitler's underground hide-out in Berlin was searched after his death there was found beside his bed a set of German architectural magazines in perfect condition.

His long conversation with Professor Kerschner had released Hitler's spring of action. By unburdening himself, he was giving the orders to start the transformation of Linz. Yet this was at a time when Hitler's political and military intentions seemed still to be in the melting-pot, with an outbreak of war far from inevitable. There was still no grand strategy, no overall plan of conquest, only the testing of his strength of will against the weakness of Britain and France. Yet deep inside him Hitler knew that his dream of Linz as the greatest cultural centre in Europe could only be achieved when Europe had been conquered. Launching the Linz project was Hitler's own acceptance within himself that he was determined on war. And he did so six months before Neville Chamberlain flew back to England with his piece of paper, crying: 'Peace in our time!'

*

The mass looting of Europe's art treasures by the Nazi leaders was on a scale unprecedented in history, the ancient barbarians preferring to satisfy their lust for destruction rather than acting as common thieves. Looting was carried out with typical German efficiency, planned beforehand and ruthlessly executed. The most avid and ostentatious plunderer in the public mind was Hermann Goering, a man in the throes of a passion for possessing, wanting to admire in private what was desired by the multitude shut outside. Goering boasted of his purchases, continually admired them, was shameless in his demands for presents from a host of sycophants. He filled Karinhall, his estate near Berlin, and his other residences with paintings, tapestries, statuary, porcelain and every other beautiful thing he could lay his pudgy hands on. His art collection was estimated to be wor th sixty million pounds at today's values.

He was outstripp d by Hitler who, quietly and without seeking any of Goering's limelight, amassed probably the greatest personal collection the world has ever known, valued at well over a hundred million pounds.

Unlike Goering, who wanted a work of art because it was beautiful, Hitler showed little interest once it had passed into his possession. Throughout the war his demand for paintings to hang on his own walls was extremely modest. Instead he preferred to store them away in dark rooms, in air-raid shelters, and deep inside salt-mines when reasons of safety compelled it. A great masterpiece was not to him a thing in itself but only a small component in a grandiose plan for glorification and settling old debts. Hitler passionately wanted certain great works not for themselves but because they were great and had to be obtained for Linz if his vision was to be realized. At times Goering was able to outwit him but mainly Hitler got what he wanted because he was the Fuehrer and had first choice of everything that was going.

Until 1938 Hitler had been a private collector of paintings through the guidance of his pet photographer, Heinrich Hoffmann, whose artistic tastes were as stunted as Hitler's own. Both men fervently admired the florid cliché-ridden nineteenth-century German painters and, if they had been Englishmen, 'The Stag At Bay' would have held pride of place in their homes. Hoffmann fully supported the exhibition of degenerate art held in Munich in 1937, encouraging Hitler in his worst excesses. After his go-ahead on Linz, Hitler stopped collecting for himself except for a few paintings that took his fancy. Everything that came into his hands was earmarked for Linz. He decided at an early stage not to select definitely those paintings or other works of arts which would be placed in the Linz museums but to amass as great a collection as possible and sort them out after Europe had been conquered. The best would go to Linz when the museums had been built and what was left over would be shared out amongst other museums throughout the Greater Reich. In this way he could also act as a benefactor to all the occupied countries.

The first step towards creating a new Linz was the drawing up of building plans, a task close to Hitler's heart. He appointed a team of architects to put down on paper their personal visions, which were all submitted directly to him. He examined them, threw them away, and then announced what he wanted. As befits a powerful dictator, his ideas were always on a grand scale. In the case of Linz, they included moving the railway station at least three miles to the south, a proposition dismissed by Hitler as a mere detail. As for the town's recently re-named Hermann Goering steelworks, Hitler diplomatically refrained from declaring himself—though there was little chance that the buildings would remain untouched.

By far the most important single factor in Hitler's plan was the design of the Fuehrermuseum, destined to be greater than the Louvre, the National Gallery, or the Metropolitan Museum in New York. After telling an architect named Roderich Frick exactly what he wanted in great detail, Hitler announced that he was to be honoured by becoming the designer of the Fuehrermuseum. Frick was somewhat hampered by the knowledge that Hitler was demanding a colonnaded façade over 160 yards long without any central accent, not unlike the Haus fuer Deutsche Kunst in Munich. The vault of the main hall was to rest on piers along the inside façade wall. Five years later Dr Hermann Voss, the newly appointed Director of the Fuehrermuseum, criticized the design and was tartly told by Frick that it was what the Fuehrer wanted and there was nothing he could have done about it. In designing a building as a home for great master-pieces, Hitler at no time consulted Voss or any other of Germany's many art experts, refusing to risk the sound of a single voice that might utter doubts concerning his personal vision.

In the years to come Germany was to achieve great victories followed by even greater defeats. But no matter how much her fortunes wavered, the work of designing a new and greater Linz went on unceasingly on paper, the first bricks and mortar having to wait until victory was finally achieved on all fronts. In order to demonstrate that the town had a special place in his limited affections, Hitler made a personal gift to Professor Kerschner's Provincial Museum of a number of paintings by artists of the German Romantic School, even including some of his beloved Spitzwegs. More and more Hitler saw the new Linz as glorifying Austro-Bavarian culture against the degenerate sophistication that emanated from Vienna, but he was not unaware that the rest of the town also must be transformed if harmony was to be achieved with its glittering centre. To this end, Hitler ordered an exhaustive study of every aspect of the town's life, the people as well as the buildings. He gave this task to one of his many Research and Planning Sections with orders that all reports, no matter how trivial, were to be sent to him for approval. When the war ended, the Allies found Hitler's private library buried deep in the Alt Aussee salt-mine and amongst its contents were scores of fully detailed architectural drawings of the many buildings that were to be built in Linz. There was also a 75-page bound, typewritten report, lavishly illustrated with statistical charts, the result of putting the town under a microscope.

As the architects, town-planners, sociologists and snoopers came and went, Linz became curious, the inevitable rumours gathering momentum amongst the townspeople. They watched the special Office of Building being installed, patiently answered the many questions put to them, and slowly began to grasp the immensity of the grandeur that was to be thrust upon them, whether they wanted it or not. One wry joke which rapidly circulated said that Munich was the city of *Bewegung* (the beginning of the Nazi movement) but Linz had become the city of *Bodenbewegung* (earthquakes). If a secret vote could have

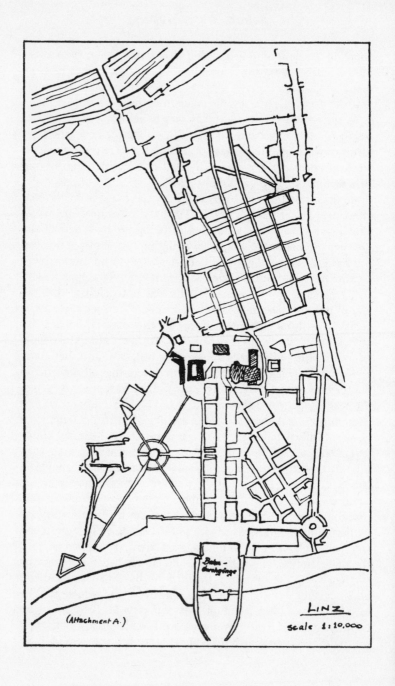

(Attachment A.)

LINZ

scale 1:10,000

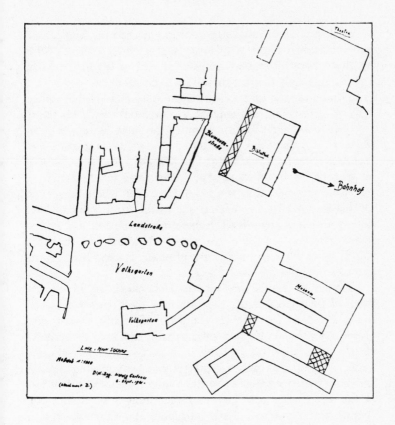

Two sketch maps of the new Linz, drawn in September 1941. These were found by American art experts buried with other Linz records in the salt-mine at Alt Aussee. The plan opposite shows the main square in the centre, the railway station at the bottom, and the proposed library on the axis of the approach to the station been taken without risk to those who participated, Linz would have declared by a vast majority that it wished the Fuehrer had been born a thousand miles away. It was left to the Allies and Russia finally to grant their wish to be left alone.

In the summer that followed the Anschluss Hitler visited Italy as part of his Axis entente. He held talks with Mussolini but still found time to visit some of the most famous art galleries. It was a somewhat shattering experience as it made him realize how far he would have to go to make Linz the greatest of all art galleries. But the size of problems never deterred military dictators, otherwise they would not have been where they were. On his return Hitler contacted one of the most influential art dealers in Germany—Karl Haberstock of Berlin, the foxiest member of his profession who could tell which way the wind was blowing while it was still a puff of air. He had been selling pictures to Hitler for some years.

That Hitler should first turn to Haberstock for advice was proof of their close association. Born in 1878, Haberstock had joined the Nazi Party in 1933 and quickly found favour with Hitler after fashioning his own artistic tastes to correspond closely with what was laid down in party dogma. If Hitler's main ambition was power, Haberstock's was making money, and both men recognized the single-minded unscrupulousness of the other. The first picture Hitler bought from him was 'Venus and Amor' by Paris Bordone, the sixteenth-century Italian artist who has been described as being 'fascinated by colour and materials but whose aims remained unco-ordinated'. Perhaps it was this last quality that struck a chord with Hitler. He liked the painting, which Haberstock had purchased in London in 1928, so much that he gave him 65,000 reichsmarks for it and always kept it at Obersalzberg. Other paintings he bought from Haberstock included Van Dyck's 'Jupiter and Antiope', Canaletto's 'Santa Maria della Salute' and Rubens's 'St Peter in the Boat'. In all these pre-war purchases Hitler never paid less than 24,000 reichsmarks for any single painting.

Haberstock ran a large gallery at 59 Kurfuerstenstrasse in Berlin and also maintained a branch in London until the day Hitler decided to invade Poland. In his dealings with the

Fuehrer he was shrewd enough not to demand exorbitant percentages for his commission, but as the sums involved were usually vast, his own profits were handsome. Until he incurred the enmity of Dr Voss when the latter was appointed Director of the Fuehrermuseum in March 1943, Haberstock sold over a hundred paintings to Hitler which were stored away as part of the Linz collections. Outstanding amongst them were Watteau's masterpiece 'La Danse', for which Hitler paid 900,000 reichsmarks, and Boecklin's 'Italian Villa', somewhat reduced at 675,000 reichsmarks. As a favourite of Hitler's, Haberstock was given considerable freedom to travel through the occupied countries during the war and was afforded every possible help by German military units. When his Berlin gallery was bombed late in the war, he was able to move to a baron's castle at Aschbach. Though life struck him some blows, he always bounced back.

Haberstock taught himself to understand Hitler's artistic taste better than Hitler did himself. The fruits of this knowledge he expressed in a letter to a Paris art dealer after France had been overrun, outlining what sort of paintings were most in demand in Germany, particularly in regard to the Linz collection. He placed them in four categories:

1. German masters of the 15th, 16th and 18th centuries, and the Romantics of the 19th century, including Truebner. Also such Rhenish masters as Januarius Zick, Heinsius and Schall.

[Few people consider them of any importance today.]

2. French artists such as Poussin, Claude Lorrain, the Fontainebleau school (but mainly Primaticcio). No interest in Renoir, Monet, Manet, etc., but would like Boucher if genuinely signed canvases. Also Fragonard and Watteau, even though they are nearly unobtainable.

3. Italian masters from the Sienese to the Venetians of the 18th century. Above all, those of the 15th and 16th centuries, including Bellini, Titian and Bordone. In the 18th century Tiepolo, Guardi and both Canalettos are preferred. No schoolpieces but works by the masters themselves.

4. Netherlands masters, including Dutch of the 17th century and Flemish of the 16th and 17th centuries. Above all, Rubens, preferably painted sketches on wood and landscapes. Still-life painters of Holland and Flanders are also of interest.

When he was summoned by Hitler after his visit to Italy, Haberstock found the Fuehrer not only talking frankly about his plans for Linz, but also for once prepared to listen to advice. As always, anxious to turn any situation to his own advantage, Haberstock shrewdly realized the possibilities of having a man building up the Linz collection who would be for ever in his debt. He reassured Hitler that Linz could become the greatest cultural centre in Europe if that was what the Fuehrer wanted. Haberstock added that he did not decry the great Italian collections, in fact, he thought they were amongst the finest in Europe, but Germany still had one to equal them. When Hitler asked him which, Haberstock replied, The Dresden Art Gallery. Then, almost as an afterthought, he added sadly that it was so unfortunate that its Director, Dr Hans Posse, whom he, Karl Haberstock, humbly considered to be the greatest museum expert in Germany, should have just lost his position through some trifling difference with a local party official.

Hitler rose superbly to the bait manipulated so craftily by this cunning fisherman. He stormed off to Dresden, ranted and raved at Gauleiter Mutschmann for his stupidity in sacking a man of such proven calibre, and promptly reinstated Dr Posse, who was as bewildered as anyone by this dramatic intervention. But he was also grateful to Hitler, even though he was completely disinterested in politics and had no desire to join the Nazi Party, advantageous as that might be in the new climate existing in Germany.

Hans Posse had worked in art galleries all his life. Born the son of a well-known archivist in the city, he was appointed Director of the Dresden Art Gallery in 1913 when still a young man. He speedily built for himself a solid reputation and purchased many paintings from art dealer Haberstock, the two men being close business acquaintances, if not friends. Haberstock had summed up Posse as a man of great talent who was also honest enough to feel he was bound to fulfil any moral debts he had incurred. If Posse was given the Linz job, Haberstock was going to make sure he knew who had first suggested him.

Hitler stayed long enough in Dresden to have several talks with Posse. He did not reveal his plans for Linz at once but he was so impressed by the other man's devotion to his work and forceful energy that he decided to confide in him. Posse had no great liking for what Hitler stood for in Germany but he felt grateful to him, as his dismissal from the Dresden Art Gallery after more than twenty-five years as Director had been a painful blow. As Hitler outlined his plans for Linz Posse's eyes gleamed, for he saw the opportunities it would create. He knew at once that scruples would be unimportant if he was given the once-in-a-lifetime chance of building up such a collection. Like many others, he was prepared to shut his eyes to what was happening outside his own particular world.

Hitler left Dresden without committing himself. But back in Berlin he talked enthusiastically about Posse to Haberstock, who then knew he was backing the right horse. Posse would get the job and Karl Haberstock would be given preference over other art dealers. What Haberstock could not foresee was that the horse he was backing would not last the course.

Further talks were held between Hitler and Dr Posse. The latter was quick to see that Hitler was dissatisfied with his past purchases, the glories of the Italian galleries having raised doubts whether what he owned was of any quality. Quick to press an advantage, Posse suggested it was time the Fuehrer reorganized his system of buying works of art. Realizing the influence possessed by Heinrich Hoffman, Posse hinted that the man might be a great photographer but that didn't mean he knew a great deal about the best paintings for museums. Posse talked on, while Hitler listened, of making Linz not just the centre of Austro-Bavarian culture but as a place for bringing together every culture in Western Europe. Hitler could recognize a fellow-dreamer but he was not entirely carried away. He insisted that in any future plans, his beloved nineteenth-century German painters must be well to the fore. Tactfully Posse did not argue the point.

By June 1939 Hitler had made up his mind. The man charged with the sacred duty of creating the greatest art collection the world has ever known in the name of Adolf Hitler was to be Hans Posse. On 26 June from Obersalzberg the Fuehrer issued his proclamation:

> I commission Dr Hans Posse, Director of the Dresden Art Gallery, to build up the new art museums for Linz.
> All Party and State services are ordered to assist Dr Posse in fulfilment of his mission.

On the same day Martin Bormann, the Fuehrer's private secretary, sent a letter to Dr Lammers, head of the Reich Chancellery in Berlin. It said:

> On behalf of the Fuehrer I wish to inform you that he has asked the Director of the Dresden Art Gallery, Dr Hans Posse, to build up the new Linz Art Museum. The Fuehrer wishes that Dr Posse for the time being receives 10,000 reichsmarks for travel and other expenses. For his work with the new Linz Art Museum, Dr Posse shall receive 1,000 reichsmarks per month expense [s] ... beginning 1 July, 1939.
> Heil Hitler!

Copies of this letter were sent to Gauleiter Buerckel in Vienna and Gauleiter Eigruber in the Upper Danube, as Austria, the first country to be occupied by the Nazis, was the obvious first field of operations for Dr Posse. These were not the last letters concerning Linz to be signed by Bormann. During the next six years he was to be the main link between Hitler and those working on the Linz project.

Other steps were rapidly taken. Hitler ordered a special commission to be set up to run the project under the title 'Sonderauftrag Linz' ('Linz Special Mission'). Its activities were classified as secret and no public mention was permitted without Hitler's personal approval. Nor was any reference to be made publicly to any pictures obtained for Linz, the later sole exceptions being Breughel's 'The Hay Harvest', previously owned by Prince Lobkowitz of Prague, and Makart's 'The Plague in Florence', announced as a gift to the Fuehrer from the Duce.

The stage was now set. The machinery now existed for gathering together the greatest art collection ever, either by looting, confiscation or forced sale. Other experts were appointed under Posse's leadership. Now Hitler could turn his eyes to his homeland—Austria. He did so with some eagerness for he had many scores to settle with its capital, Vienna.

CHAPTER TWO

The Machine is Created

As soon as the Austrian people had voted by an overwhelming majority for Adolf Hitler to be their Fuehrer, some of the finest paintings in Europe, part of Vienna's museum and private collections, were his for the taking. Yet Hitler was in no hurry to lay hands on them. He ordered the confiscation of Jewish collections but that was an automatic part of his racial policy and Nazi officials in Vienna were instructed to store this vast plunder until further word came from Berlin. Hitler was determined that the Linz collection should be built up in systematic fashion. As with the later settlement of the Jewish problem by slaughtering millions of people, looting must be properly organized and efficiently carried out. For more than a year after the Anschluss the great art collections of Vienna remained in the city while the machinery to receive, catalogue and distribute the plunder was rapidly assembled.

The Sonderauftrag Linz was a typically German organization. It had its network of command, its divisions and subdivisions. Though its ultimate aim was a vision of Adolf Hitler's that had to be put into cold storage as long as the war lasted, preparations still proceeded methodically with no loose ends left untied. It is part of the German character to create even dreams in a painstaking fashion.

Where the Sonderauftrag differed from other Nazi organizations was in one important respect. The man at the top was Hitler himself, knowing everything that was going on and making the ultimate decisions himself. Linz was to be his creation and not even the growing demands of fighting a war on several fronts were to loosen his hands from the reins. Hitler chose Munich as the Sonderauftrag's headquarters because it was the birthplace of the Nazi movement and conveniently near Berchtesgaden. He ordered that the capacious air-raid shelters under the city's Fuehrerbau should be used for storing any work of art being considered for Linz. Every four or six weeks he visited the Fuehrerbau, when the treasures started pouring in, to inspect the latest haul and make his own selections. He read every report and by 1941 those working in the Sonderauftrag were being instructed to type all reports in treble spacing on thick white paper because of the Fuehrer's fading eyesight.

If Hitler dominated the Sonderauftrag, the undisputed second-in-command was Martin Bormann. In 1939 he was little known even in Germany, a colourless personality, self-effacing and nondescript, whose power was to grow steadily as Hitler leaned on him more and more. Bormann was the perfect secretary. He made himself indispensable to Hitler by studying his every wish and command. He quickly recognized the emotional importance that the Linz project held for his master and always treated it as a priority, handling its affairs with great energy. All the correspondence concerning Linz went through his office and a great deal of it Bormann dealt with personally. On his appointment Hans Posse had been placed in charge of all the Linz collections and was given a great deal of independence but Bormann still watched his activities closely, even though he admired Posse's energy and drive. Bormann acted as Hitler's extra eyes and voice, and in the case of the Linz library issued instructions that no books were to be bought without his prior approval. In the perpetual feud between Hitler and Goering for possession of the choicest works of art, Bormann acted for his master against Alfred Rosenberg, whose Einsatzstab or administration, set up in Paris to loot that city's vast artistic wealth, was dominated by the fat

Reich Marshal. It was Bormann who suggested to Hitler that he be given photographs of all works of art collected by the Einsatzstab before any decision was made as to their allocation, an attempt to ensure that Hitler always had first choice which was only partially successful.

Bormann's own secretary, Dr Hanssen, was also active in Linz affairs, mainly as the intermediary between Bormann and Reich Minister Dr Lammers, who administered its finances. As President of the Reich Chancellery, Lammers had offices at 6 Vossstrasse in Berlin. From there he paid the Sonderauftrag's salaries and bills, passed expense accounts which were liberal, and issued numerous orders for the confiscation of works of art. Lammers also made large sums available for Posse and his Linz agents to draw on during their buying trips outside Germany.

In the field of obtaining works of art, Posse dominated the Sonderauftrag. He was an indefatigable traveller, never spared himself and wasted no time in building up a network of purchasing agents as the countries of Europe fell into Nazi hands. Given the title of 'Sonderbeauftrager' ('Special Envoy') Posse was responsible for paintings, which included statuary and tapestries, armour and coins. At a later date his various jobs were distributed between three men, a remarkable tribute to Posse's extraordinary abilities.

Other members of the Sonderauftrag had, however, important roles to play. The task of obtaining rare books and manuscripts for the Linz library was given to Dr Friedrich Wolffhardt. Born at Landshut in December 1899, Wolffhardt operated from an office in the Munich Fuehrerbau. He was an active Nazi, later becoming an S.S. Captain. Tall, blond and blue-eyed, Wolffhardt was extremely efficient, keeping the records of the vast number of books he had obtained always in perfect order. He was rarely troubled about maintaining legalities when it came to plundering existing libraries. He preferred plundering and looting whereas Posse liked to pay money for what he obtained, even though the price was seldom a fair one and the seller had been forced to part with a thing of beauty that he had wanted to keep.

Posse's second-in-command in building up the Linz coin

collection was Dr Fritz Dworschak, who was later to be promoted to head of the department. Dworschak was an art historian who had always specialized in coins, and before 1938 held the post of Curator of Coins under Ritter von Loehr at the Kunsthistorisches Institut in Vienna. Also a strong Nazi, Dworschak was a close friend of Seyss-Inquart and the Anschluss brought him rapid promotion. Baldur von Schirach, a high-ranking Nazi administrator, appointed him Director of all the collections at the Kunsthistorisches Institut, the first man ever to hold such a post. Dworschak immediately embarked on a policy of sacking all experts and other employees not known to be pro-Nazi and replacing them with his own appointments, thus transforming this famous institute into yet another Nazi organization. His subsequent appointment to the Sonderauftrag Linz was a further extension of his power and influence.

Two other men deserve mention. Placed in charge of the Linz clearing-house at the Munich Fuehrerbau was Hans Reger, a minor party functionary who was an architect by profession. He employed a Munich photographer by the name of Rudolf Himpsl to photograph all works of art delivered to the Fuehrerbau. The other was Dr Rudolf Oertel, who had been Posse's assistant at the Dresden Art Gallery. When Posse received his Linz appointment, he took Oertel with him to help him collect paintings for Linz. Then about thirty-four, Oertel had strong Nazi sympathies, though he respected Posse's abilities too much to resent the fact that he did not share them.

These were the men who had the main task of launching the Sonderauftrag Linz. None of them was old, all had great drive and organizing ability. Death was to take its toll so that others had to be drawn in to play important roles. But at the beginning it was the three party leaders—Hitler, Bormann, and Lammers —plus Hans Posse and his experts who set out to lay the foundations for the unequalled glorification of Adolf Hitler. And as the Nazis swept through Europe, it seemed that there was nothing to stand in their way. Nothing except the rivalry of Goering, until his stock began to fall as rapidly as his Luftwaffe planes spiralled earthwards.

*

The machinery existed and now it was time to put it into action.

In Austria the obvious first target was the Rothschilds. Baron Louis von Rothschild was the richest man in the country. He owned a bank—S. M. Rothschild und Soehne—and was one of the largest land-owners in Central Europe. He also possessed large investments in the mining, textile and chemical industries. During the economic depression of the 1930s Baron Louis had given up his huge mansion in Vienna's Prinz Eugen-strasse but the Rothschilds still owned their palace in Theresianumgasse which was a treasure-house, containing a vast collection of works of art from the periods of Louis XIV, XV and XVI, including four Van Loons commissioned by Madame de Pompadour.

Three days after the Germans occupied Vienna, Baron Louis was arrested by the Gestapo, though they politely waited for him to finish a meal when they called. The various Rothschild mansions were stripped bare and hundreds of items belonging to Baron Louis and his brother, Alphonse, were confiscated, including *objets d'art*, coins, rare books, armour, and beautiful pieces of furniture. They were to form part of more than four thousand works of art belonging to various branches of the Rothschild family which were to fall into Hitler's hands and be stored away for his Linz museums. In Vienna Baron Louis was robbed without being at any time offered a penny compensation by the Nazis, though they did allow him to leave Austria a year later after a colossal ransom had been paid, which included the transfer of all ordinary Rothschild assets in the country.

The Gestapo made further raids, seizing other Jewish collections in and outside Vienna. Everything they took away was sorted and catalogued, then stored in the city, classified by Hitler's orders as 'safeguarded property'. No attempt was made to move any of this great wealth into Germany and as the Nazi caches grew full to overflowing, demanding that more storage space be found for large canvases, huge tapestries and bulky pieces of furniture, the Nazi administration in Vienna began to wonder when it would be rid of its unwelcome responsibility.

But still Hitler stayed silent, waiting for his Sonderauftrag to be ready to start operations.

In the late spring of 1939 Gauleiter Josef Buerckel was moved to write to Berlin from Vienna, summoning all his courage to inquire when some decision could be expected about the vast amount of plunder he was still safeguarding. He received an answer from Bormann on 24 July, sixteen months after the Anschluss. Bormann informed him curtly that 'The Fuehrer alone will decide . . .' but added:

> Gallery Director Dr Posse of Dresden has been asked by the Fuehrer to inspect the safeguarded art treasures and to make a report together with photographic records.

This was just four weeks after Posse's appointment to Linz had been announced. He travelled to Vienna in the September to appraise the booty, but there was so much to be seen that it took him several weeks to inspect all the plunder in the various storage depots. He was ruthless in his judgements, never hesitating to cast aside anything he did not think worthy of forming part of the Linz collection. It was not until 20 October that he submitted his first detailed report to Bormann in Berlin. He wrote:

Dear Reichsleiter,

Following instructions from the Fuehrer, I have informed myself concerning the museums in Ostmark and I beg to submit to you the enclosed:

1. Suggestion for the distribution of paintings confiscated from Jewish property in Vienna.

2. Short reports on the provincial museums in Ostmark.

I have communicated instructions to Vienna that the inspection of the material remaining from confiscated property (sculpture, applied art, graphics, armour, Gobelins, etc.) should be continued as well as the inspection of merely safeguarded property so that here too a plan of distribution can be set up and submitted to the Fuehrer for decision. . . .

The 'enclosed' included a list of 269 carefully selected paintings, the best of the confiscated Jewish collections. Posse proposed that these collections should not be broken up excessively 'especially in consideration of the art museum, which is to be built at Linz'. He suggested that the distribution of the paintings be limited to the most important museums in Austria but with Linz exercising its right of first preference. Of the 269 paintings, Posse proposed that 122 should go to Linz; forty-four to the Kunsthistorisches Institut in Vienna, made up of ten old masters, eight of the English school, and twenty-six by French artists, including a life-size portrait of Madame de Pompadour by Boucher; thirteen to the Oesterreichische Galerie in Vienna, all of which it had requested, twenty-five to the Ferdinandeum, the Provincial Museum in Innsbruck, and only five to the Provincial Gallery at Graz, the country's second largest city.

The remaining sixty paintings, proposed Posse, should be kept back in reserve for the Linz collection if later the Fuehrer decided he wanted them.

The seizing of these Jewish collections in Vienna was the first large-scale plundering by the Nazis, though Austria was technically not an occupied country but a willing part of the Greater Reich. Therefore it was of some significance that Hitler was proposing to grab two-thirds of these paintings for himself. His share was more than double that given to the four most important museums in Austria.

The 122 paintings proposed for Linz included twenty-two German paintings, some by the nineteenth-century Romantics but including a Holbein and a Lucas Cranach; three of the Netherlands sixteenth-century school—by Mostaert, Pieter Coeck van Aelst and Antonio Moro; eleven by Flemish painters, including three Van Dycks, two Jan Fyts, and two by David Teniers the Younger; forty Dutch old masters, including Rembrandt's portrait of Anthonis Coopal, painted in 1635, two Franz Hals, a Jan Steen, three Van Ostades, two landscapes by Jacob van Ruisdael and a Van de Capelle; eleven Italian paintings, including two Tintorettos and two by Francesco Guardi; sixteen French paintings, among them two Fragonards, two

Bouchers, a Nattier and a Largillière; and a solitary English portrait, Romney's 'Lady Forbes'.

It was obvious that Posse held no high opinion of English paintings. He allowed three more Romneys, a Gainsborough and a Reynolds to go to the Kunsthistorisches Institut.

Posse felt some pride in submitting his first detailed report but if he thought these long lists of great paintings were to be subjected just to the routine of a rubber-stamp approval, he was quickly disillusioned. Hitler examined Posse's proposed distribution carefully. He was not pleased to read that as many as fifty-seven out of 269 of Vienna's great paintings were to re-remain in the city. He reached for his pen and began to revise Posse's lists. By the time he had finished, nearly twenty paintings, scheduled for either of the two Viennese museums, had been switched to the Linz list. His disapproval was conveyed to Posse in a tart letter from Bormann that he received on his return to Dresden:

> The Fuehrer has looked through the lists you have sent him. He does not agree to your proposals for Vienna; it will be sufficient if Vienna receives the Boucher, and those paintings and art objects which the Fuehrer had previously agreed upon. Vienna already has enough works of art and it is entirely unnecessary to enlarge these collections. It is right to make use of these art objects for Linz or as a foundation for other collections.
>
> I ask you to limit the distribution plan for Vienna in accordance with the Fuehrer's decision.

Later events were to show that Hitler's bias was not confined solely to Vienna. All the museums throughout Germany, including Posse's beloved Dresden Art Gallery, were to suffer because of Hitler's determination that the best of everything must be reserved for Linz. Throughout the war years German museums obtained few acquisitions of any importance.

Posse made a second journey to Vienna in December 1939. On the 14th he sent a further report to Bormann in Berlin, the paintings he listed being divided into two categories: the confiscated, which was property owned by Jews or other enemies of the State, and the safeguarded. But these fine distinctions meant nothing as the Nazis had no intention of returning any work of art once they had laid their hands on it. Posse reported that he was continuing to examine valuable works of art which had been stored in caches outside Vienna. He added that further collections had been added since his first visit, and waxed enthusiastic about the Bondy collection and that of the Polish Count Lanckoronski. He told Bormann:

> They include important antique marbles in addition to early Italian paintings. These, with the large stock of art objects from Jewish property, are being inspected and inventoried. This should be finished in the next few weeks so that, in the course of January, I shall be in a position to inspect these stocks too, and to submit proposals as to their distribution. The result of the work done is extremely valuable and will be of great importance, especially for the Art Museum in Linz.

Posse was also expanding his ideas. He saw no reason why they should stop at stripping the paintings from the walls of Jewish homes when the walls could be stripped also if they were valuable. In the same letter to Bormann he wrote:

> I further request that the Sicherheitsdienst [Security Service] in Vienna be instructed to dismantle the two remaining rooms in the Palais Rothschild (in Theresianumgasse): the so-called 'Hague Salon' and the 'Museum Hall', containing precious old wainscoting and leather wallpapers, a Gothic stone chimney, a Renaissance chimney and Renaissance portals and doors.

If others did not suffer as savagely as the Jewish families, they still suffered. One such victim was Prince Schwarzenberg, an extensive land and property owner, who included a palace in Vienna amongst his possessions. He was ordered by the Nazis to return to Germany and enlist in the Wehrmacht. The Prince refused and had all his property confiscated, the best of his art collection being taken by Hitler for Linz.

Posse's activities in Vienna had been the subject of much comment by other Nazis in the city. Realizing that he operated with Bormann's authority and had a direct line of communication with the Fuehrer, they were not slow to appreciate that here was a means by which they could curry favour for themselves. Vienna possessed a large collection of beautiful Gobelin tapestries, two of the most favoured sets depicting the victories of Alexander the Great. One set was openly 'borrowed' by the traitorous Seyss-Inquart for hanging in the lobby of the Reich Chancellery in Berlin, though nobody in Vienna expected to see it again. The second set, which was even more valuable, was secretly taken away at night and sent to Hitler by Gauleiter Buerckel, as a token of his tremendous admiration of and devotion to his Fuehrer whose victories would be even more glorious than Alexander's. It was a gift much appreciated by Hitler.

Working in Vienna at this time but as yet not a member of the Sonderauftrag Linz was Dr Leopold Ruprecht. Born in Vienna in 1890, he was a child in the city to which Hitler came as a youth with his burning artistic aspirations. Now Ruprecht had risen to the post of Curator of Armour at the Kunsthistorisches Institut. Like his colleague, Dr Dworschak, Ruprecht was a fervent Nazi.

As soon as the first Jewish collections had been confiscated, he was called in by Seyss-Inquart to examine the armour, working directly under Dr Kajetan Muehlmann, a protégée of Seyss-Inquart. He kept the large Rothschild collection of armour in Post Sparknasse and in Neue Berg. His methods were invariably brutal: he preferred straightforward plundering to any other means of acquisition. If he had to buy a piece of armour, he permitted the presentation of the bill but rarely paid. When the Dorotheum, the famous Viennese auction-house, received no payment from him for bills of 124,000 and 53,700 reichsmarks, it suggested that the armour in question should remain its property until the money was forthcoming. Ruprecht replied that even to consider such a suggestion was beneath his dignity. An expect in other fields besides armour and formerly employed at the Dorotheum, Ruprecht was later to become one of the most important members of the Linz organization.

Thanks to his assistance, Posse was able to send a report to Hitler via Bormann on 28 February 1941 recommending that of the 190 pieces of armour in the Rothschild collection, all but twenty inferior pieces should be earmarked for the Linz Armour Hall 'which the Fuehrer is planning to build'. Two days later Posse received Hitler's approval, this time without any alterations.

In the same report Posse was able to give details of the widespread seizure of collections of valuable coins, under the direction of Dr Fritz Dworschak. Posse outlined his plans for distributing the immensely valuable coins and medals that formed the collections of Leo Furst and Baron Louis von Rothschild. He also informed Hitler that he wished to purchase thirty-nine gold coins from the Alexander Hauser collection, which had been confiscated by the Nazis as part of Reich escape tax. The price to Hitler was 12,000 reichsmarks, a little over 300 reichsmarks per coin. This was a mockery of a price considering that Hitler was at a later date to pay 750,000 reichsmarks for German gold coins minted since 1871.

Austria was to prove the main source of the great number of valuable coins looted by Hitler. Collections held in thirteen religious foundations were confiscated, and twelve of them were situated in Austria. They included those at Klosterneuburg, Göttweig, Kremsmuenster, Lambach, St. Florian, Schloegl, Wilhering and St Peter in Salzburg. The total haul was so tremendous that Hitler decided to set up a special coin cabinet at Linz, as part of the Fuehrermuseum. He issued a decree from Berlin, stating that the corner-stone of the coin cabinet would be the coin and medal collection of Klosterneuberg in Lower Austria. Clause 3 of the decree stated:

For scientific inventorising and uniform handling and disposition, all coin and medal collections seized since March 13, 1938 (the date of Hitler's arrival in Vienna) and in the Alps and Danube Reichsgauen are to be turned over to the coin cabinet, even if they have been transferred already to public agencies as property or part thereof.

This was a new excuse. Previously the Nazis had announced that they were 'safeguarding' or 'taking into safe custody'. Now they were claiming the need for 'scientific inventorising' and 'uniform handling and disposition'.

*

From the day he had taken over Austria, Hitler had used his position of supreme power to bid for paintings on sale that he could not confiscate. He paid the enormous sum of 900,000 reichsmarks for Rembrandt's portrait of Henrickje Stoffels, 65,000 for Makart's large portrait of Cleopatra, 15,500 for a Madonna and Child of the Rubens school, 10,000 for Giordano's 'Venus and Mars', and 27,500 for Lenbach's portrait of Bismarck which was much to Hitler's personal taste. He also bought four mythological scenes by Rahl. The Linz records kept in Munich were to show that he purchased seventy-five works of art through the Dorotheum alone, most of them paintings.

Sometimes even Hitler was squeamish about looting in too brazen a manner. This happened in the case of the glorious masterpiece by Rubens, 'Ganymede carried off by an Eagle'. It was first seen by Dr Posse when he paid a chance visit to the restoring studio of the Oesterreichische Galerie to which the painting had been temporarily moved while the Schwarzenberg Palace was undergoing conversion into a museum. The sight of this great masterpiece aroused all his collector's passion. Posse immediately wrote to Bormann, saying that the Rubens must be obtained for the Linz collections, no matter what means had to be adopted. He pointed out that up to that date—1 February 1941—few Rubens had been obtained for Linz, an oversight that must be corrected. And he added that all that was needed was a decree of confiscation signed by the Fuehrer.

But for Hitler and Bormann the problem was not so simple. Austria was an ally, not an occupied country. The invasion of Britain had failed, and the invasion of Russia was being planned.

It was no time unduly to offend one's friends. Deciding that more subtle methods were needed, Bormann wrote back on Hitler's instructions that the Fuehrer had decided to present the Bloch-Bauer collection of porcelain—which he little admired—to the city of Vienna. As an exchange of goodwill, he was prepared to accept the Rubens. Bormann informed Posse by letter that the Fuehrer insisted on this barter for 'psychological reasons' but elaborated no further. Hitler was given his Rubens, which was entered in the Linz records simply as 'Item 1887'. It was then stored away so that no man could enjoy its great beauty.

Another magnificent work of art acquired by Hitler in Vienna was the life-size seated marble statue by Canova of Polyhymnia, the Muse of song and poetry. Though weighing a ton and a half, it gives a marvellous sense of delicacy and grace. It was begun by Canova in 1812 as a portrait of Maria-Elisa, Napoleon's sister who was given the title of Princess of Lucca. When she lost her fortune and could not pay Canova, he idealized the head, thus changing it into that of a goddess. It was given to the Emperor of Austria and eventually passed down into the hands of his granddaughter, the Princess Windischgraetz. Hitler bought it from her and for the next four years the statue was hidden in a small room at the Hohenfurth monastery, just inside the Czech border. It was discovered there by art experts attached to the American Seventh Army, covered with dust but otherwise undamaged.

Though Hitler gained many magnificent Austrian art treasures, all were to be overshadowed by one single painting. When it passed into Hitler's hands, it became one of the three or four greatest paintings out of all the vast number that finally formed the Linz collection. It was the 'Portrait of an Artist in his Studio' by the great Dutch master, Jan Vermeer, by whom there are little more than forty unquestioned canvases in the whole world. To the art world, this one was always known as the 'Czernin Vermeer', being in the possession of the German family in Vienna for many years. The richest collectors in many countries had avidly but unsuccessfully sought this superb painting, Count Czernin always refusing to part with it. It was reputed that Andrew Mellon, the American multi-millionaire, had offered six million dollars for the Vermeer, and been turned down. But rich and influential as the Mellons of this world are, they are not warlords with power over life and death.

Hitler had no ready excuse for seizing the Vermeer, the Czernin family being neither Jewish nor classifiable as enemies of the State. In addition there were no financial grounds for confiscation, as was made clear by Beyer of the Reich Finance Ministry in Berlin when he wrote thus to Bormann:

> The Oberfinanzpraesidium [Chief Treasury Office] of Vienna has notified me that the brothers Czernin at present have no tax debts. The inheritance tax for the property has not yet been ascertained. It is likely to amount to 500,000 reichsmarks.
>
> Since there are no tax arrears, the Vermeer picture, which is part of the estate, cannot be sold at auction.

But though he was without any weapon that could by any stretch be justified under one of the numerous Nazi decrees, Hitler still persevered. For once Posse did not have to convince him of the greatness of the prize. Relentless pressure was put on the Czernin family to sell, always backed with unspoken threats. Dworschak took a prominent part in turning the screw with meticulous exactitude, a pastime he readily enjoyed in between his official duties at the Kunsthistorisches Institut. The Czernin family had watched the brutal treatment meted out by the Gestapo to those who had incurred its displeasure, and knew that the threats were not idle ones. By September 1940, they were ready to yield. On the 26th Bormann was able to write in triumph to Posse in Dresden:

> We have several times discussed the Vermeer which is in the Czernin collection in Vienna. The Fuehrer himself has told you of the amount demanded for this picture, which up to now has been incredibly high.
>
> As has recently been ascertained, Count Czernin now asks for the Vermeer the sum of 1,400,000 plus taxes of 250,000

reichsmarks. The Fuehrer wants to purchase the picture and wishes you to leave for Vienna immediately in order to make the purchase contract. You are requested to contact at once in Vienna Reichsleiter von Schirach, whom I have informed. Von Schirach will assign one of his officials to accompany you to conclude the purchase agreement with Czernin, so that the affair may be rapidly settled.

'As has recently been ascertained.' Five ordinary words that could not have been given more sinister undertones, as penned by Bormann. The agreed price was ridiculously low, compared with the past offers that the Czernins had turned down. Previously one of Hitler's pet dealers, Frau Maria Dietrich, had written to him to say that she was considering bidding for the Vermeer but thought the price would be at least 2,000,000 reichsmarks. By using his own methods, Hitler had saved himself nearly a quarter of that sum.

Posse left for Vienna on 30 September and contacted Baldur von Schirach. The contract details were rapidly completed and the news that one of the world's great paintings had been forcibly purchased by Adolf Hitler was conveyed in a commonplace telegram sent by Dworschak on 11 October to Hans Reger in the Munich Fuehrerbau. It simply said: 'Arrive with picture Saturday early afternoon. Dimensions 120 cm. high by 100 cm. wide.' The Vermeer became Item 1096 in the Linz records with the notation: 'Obtained through Dr Fritz Dworschak, Vienna, 12 October 1940.'

The Vermeer's glowing beauty was hidden first in the Fuehrerbau's dark air-raid shelter and later in the greater darkness of the Alt Aussee salt-mine. The world's only reminder of its existence was the colour reproduction that appeared on the cover of the *Kunst dem Volk* in April 1943, one of the rare occasions when Hitler permitted an article to be published on his Linz collection. Its author was Heinrich Hoffmann. Only after Hitler's death were free men able to bring it up into the daylight and once more feast their eyes. Finally, the Vermeer was returned to Vienna.

CHAPTER THREE

The Vultures Swoop

Six months after signing the Munich agreement with the British and French, Hitler tore the document up. His troops moved into the rest of Czechoslovakia, meeting no resistance from the betrayed Czechs. But there was none of the wild acclamation that had greeted the Nazis and their Fuehrer in Linz and Vienna. Prague met her conquerors with a sullen silence. This was no Anschluss but the brutal subjugation of a proud people. Hitler entered Prague on 15 March 1939, staying the night at the historic Hradčany Castle. Next morning he left with a number of valuable tapestries, rolled up and furtively stuffed into the back of his car, like some hotel-guest surreptitiously stealing the establishment's inscribed towels before checking out.

In Austria Hitler had soft-pedalled the outright plundering of art treasures. The great Jewish families were fair game but elsewhere he was forced to tread warily. He had to remember that the Austrians were now part of the Greater Reich, members of the Nazi family whose sensibilities could not be treated with contempt. No such considerations hampered him in Czechoslovakia. The only truly democratic state east of the Rhine had been eliminated, and there were to be no scruples about plundering the corpse.

The Rosenberg organization of art experts trained to carry out systematic looting had still to be formed. In Czechoslovakia the task was given to the Army and S.S., whose ideas of plundering were to seize everything within reach without consideration of historic or æsthetic values. In November 1939 Deputy Reich Protector Karl Frank ordered the plundering of Prague University, and its great library was stripped of numerous paintings, statues and rare manuscripts. The Modern Art Gallery in the city was ruthlessly looted of its unique collection of nineteenth- and twentieth-century Czech paintings. The Czech National Museum was picked clean, the Nazis seized the crown jewels of the ancient Czech kings, and the priceless Gobelins tapestries in Prague's Maltese Palace were removed secretly at night. Plundering on the same scale was carried out in Bratislava and other large towns.

Hitler had no great regard for the art treasures of Eastern Europe, in which he included Czechoslovakia, and Himmler and his S.S. played only a minor role in seizing works of art for the Linz collection. They were most active in Prague, where they were able to make one of their few direct gifts. The secret police seized seven paintings by minor seventeenth-century Dutch and nineteenth-century German artists, and presented them to the Fuehrer. Reger, in Munich, entered them in his Linz records as Items 1967 to 1973.

Far more active in Czechoslovakia was Ruprecht, the armour expert, for this was a country rich in collections of armour. He plundered four great castles—Radnitz Castle, owned by Prince Lobkowitz: Konopiště Castle, owned by Archduke Franz Ferdinand; Opočno Castle, owned by Count Coloredo; and Frauenberg Castle, owned by Prince Schwarzenberg. Ruprecht reported to Bormann on the seizure of these great collections with his tongue in his cheek:

> The seizure of the total property of art objects, libraries, etc., and their transfer to Prague was undertaken on the one hand to empty the localities concerned and use them for other purposes, and on the other hand to enrich the existing art collections in Prague. This action is justified by the idea of broadening the cultural basis for the 300,000 Germans in the

Protectorate so that the German character of old Reichsland Bohemia will be emphasized and underlined.

But the needs of Prague were only secondary. Ruprecht was well aware that the Fuehrer's demands for additions to his Linz collection outweighed everything else, as became clear when these great collections were brought to the Hradčany Castle in Prague. Greatly impressed by the sight of so much historic armour and so many weapons, the Wehrmacht stepped in with the proposal that Germany's military glory be celebrated by using the entire collection to form an Army Museum in Prague, an amenity previously lacking in the city. Ruprecht wasted no time in meeting this threat. Having assured himself that Hitler had not been so far consulted as to the disposition of art treasures seized in the Protectorates of Bohemia and Moravia, he wrote to Bormann again:

> As I presume that a large part of the collections of armour from confiscated property will be of importance also to the Sonderauftrag Linz, I request, according to the instructions by the Reichsminister and the chief of the Reichskanzlei to the OKW [German High Command] concerning extension of the Fuehrer's reserve of old stores of armour, that an order be obtained allowing me to take over some objects for the purposes so desired by the Fuehrer.

Bormann was also quick to recognize the danger. The necessary authority was immediately obtained from Hitler and sent to Ruprecht, who walked into the HradčanyCastle to choose what he had called 'some objects'. He selected the cream of the collections and gave orders that the armour be conveyed to Munich. The Wehrmacht was permitted to have what was left for its Army Museum, which had been greatly impoverished before it could even open.

Due mainly to Ruprecht's efforts, the Linz armour collection had by now grown to well over 150 large pieces, as well as many smaller items. Nearly all of it had come from one of two cities, Prague or Vienna.

Hans Posse meanwhile had not been idle. With so many riches before him, his standards of what was good enough for Linz were being raised rather than lowered. Nevertheless there were some paintings in Czechoslovakia that measured up to them. The one he valued above all others was Pieter Breughel's 'The Hay Harvest'. Posse had located the painting in the Lobkowitz collection held at Radnitz Castle. He wrote to Bormann:

I have only just learned through a memorandum from the Director of the Kaiser Friedrich Museum in Berlin that the famous Lobkowitz collection in the Protectorate will be seized by the Reich. In addition to armour and *objets d'art*, the collection includes highly valuable German, Italian, Spanish, French and Netherlandish paintings, among which is 'The Hay Harvest' by Pieter Breughel the Elder which the Kaiser Friedrich Museum has been negotiating for some time prior to the confiscation proceedings.

It would be advisable to suggest to the Reichsprotektor von Neurath that an inspection of the Radnitz items be arranged so that claims may be filed in time by the German museums and, above all, by the Fuehrermuseum.

Never slow to take a hint, Bormann immediately issued instructions to von Neurath as coming from Hitler. Posse was given first choice of the Lobkowitz collection, selecting the Breughel and a number of other paintings. 'The Hay Harvest' was sent to him in Dresden, then on to Munich, where it was entered as Linz Item 2124.

Yet another great Czech masterpiece was even more easily obtained by Posse after others had been struggling to gain possession. This was the famous altarpiece of the Hohenfurth monastery near Krumau in the Sudetenland. It consisted of nine panels, in three rows, each about four feet square. Painted about 1350, the altarpiece is the work of an unknown artist, invariably referred to by historians as the 'Master of Hohenfurth'. It ranks amongst the greatest works of art inspired by man's religious beliefs. The first row of panels depicts the Annunciation, Birth of Christ, and the Three Magi; the second row, Christ on the Mount of Olives, Christ Carrying the Cross and Pietà; and the third row, the Resurrection, Pentecost and Ascension.

Before Hitler threatened their independence the Czechs considered the Hohenfurth altarpiece not only a great religious work of art but also a national treasure. In 1938, when the Sudetenland was threatened, the Czech Government wasted no time in moving the altarpiece to Prague, using as a pretext that it needed cleaning and restoring. Work on the altarpiece was started and was still going on when the Nazis entered Prague. The Sudetenland, which considered itself as German as any part of Germany, now clamoured for the return of the altarpiece. In April 1939 Gauleiter Eigruber of the Sudetenland ordered that the restoration work be stopped and the altarpiece returned to its rightful home. But the Nazis in Prague saw no reason why they should jump when Eigruber shouted and it was only after thirteen months of wrangling that the altarpiece was returned to Hohenfurth on a lorry specially adapted for the purpose.

Eigruber had carried out the wishes of the Sudetenland people but he saw no reason why he should still observe them when he could so easily manipulate the situation for his personal gain. Like all Nazis below the top strata of the party, he was always seeking ways to lift himself up on to the last rung of the ladder. He appreciated the need to be looked on favourably by the Fuehrer and so decided that though the altarpiece still technically belonged to the Hohenfurth monastery, there was no reason why it shouldn't become a birthday offering to Hitler. Meanwhile until that glorious day came, the work of restoration could go on. To this end, Eigruber consulted the best experts in both Berlin and Vienna.

He made his move on 17 April 1941, three days before Hitler's fifty-second birthday. Eigruber sent an urgent telegram to Dr Hanssen, Bormann's secretary, informing him that the Hohenfurth alterpiece had been confiscated. Fully aware that he would have to justify this sudden action, Eigruber had his reasons ready. He claimed that the Hohenfurth monastery had been a centre of rebellion during the Czech regime and still continued to be so after the establishment of the Protectorate. He accused its inmates of listening to foreign-radio broadcasts. Finally, Eigruber reported that he had discovered a number of homosexual intrigues of such a horrible nature that they justified removing the altarpiece away from such a polluted atmosphere. If these reasons seemed blatantly transparent, it must have been because Eigruber as a Gauleiter was not accustomed to having to justify his actions.

He followed up his telegram with a letter to Bormann which grandiloquently stated:

I ask you, dear Herr Reichsleiter, to tell the Fuehrer on his birthday that the Hohenfurth altarpiece has been confiscated and is now the property of Germany.

To ingratiate himself even further, Eigruber revealed that for some time he had been collecting old prints of Linz, some from Italy, some from private sources, but most of them from art shops in Vienna. This labour of love he also wished to present to the Fuehrer to mark his birthday.

Bormann's reply was brusque enough to be insulting. On the same day that he received Eigruber's letter, he wrote back:

I immediately informed the Fuehrer about the contents of your telegram of yesterday's date. The Fuehrer's expert for the new Linz Gallery, Director Dr Posse, has been notified through me. He is to advise the Fuehrer whether the altarpiece should remain in Hohenfurth or if later on it should come to the new Linz Gallery.

As you have already been informed, the Fuehrer has declined to receive all visitors not absolutely necessary on the occasion of his birthday.

I ask you, therefore, to forward your birthday present to me.

With the upstart Eigruber satisfactorily put in his place, Bormann wrote to Posse, enclosing photographs of the altarpiece and informing him that it was his decision as to whether it was received as part of the Linz collection. Posse wasted no time in informing Bormann that he wanted the altarpiece but even he felt compelled to produce excuses to justify what was blatant thieving. He wrote to Bormann:

The nine panels of the Hohenfurth Master, coming from the 14th century, are amongst the oldest and most famous products of German painting. . . . In Hohenfurth, which is very much off the road, they were withheld from the public, and these unique pieces of German painting will be much better cared for in a public museum than in a religious foundation which for a long time has had no importance.

To pluralize Shakespeare, methinks they all did protest too much.

But the Czechs did not lose every battle against the Nazis to retain their national art treasures. Their most notable victory was the long struggle for the Lobkowitz collection of musical instruments, plus a library of historic music documents kept in five special cabinets and a number of portraits of composers. They had been confiscated with the rest of the contents of Radnitz Castle but neither Posse nor Ruprecht had expressed any interest and this valuable and unique collection had been moved to the University of Prague for safekeeping.

There it remained until late in the war when Dr Friedrich Wolffhardt, in charge of building up the Linz library, discovered that the Lobkowitz music collection had been overlooked. He decided it was worthy to be added to Linz. Because of Allied air attacks Wolffhardt had moved out of the Munich Fuehrerbau late in 1943 to the Villa Castiglione at Grundlsee and it was from there he wrote to the Chief of the Gestapo in Prague on 16 August 1944. Wolffhardt pointed out that some of the paintings owned by Prince Lobkowitz had already been annexed by Dr Posse for Linz and he saw no reason why the music collection shouldn't be treated likewise. He requested information regarding its legal status and asked for a stock-list to be sent to him.

Wolffhardt had to wait over a fortnight before he received a reply. A short letter informed him that the music collection had been handed over to the Property Office of the German Ministry for Bohemia and his request had been forwarded to them. Hearing no more, Wolffhardt again wrote to the Gestapo on 23 September, asking the reasons for the long silence. Again he was told that his original letter had been forwarded to the Ministry and he must contain his soul in patience. He finally received a letter on 6 October, informing him that the Lobkowitz music collection had been officially 'on loan to the Reich' for the past two years but had remained in Prague because of national cultural interests, a decision that owed much to the influence of Professor Swoboda of the city's main museum.

The Property Office was in two minds. It was well aware that Wolffhardt's authority came direct from the Fuehrer but it had no desire to help him. On 11 October an official wrote to Wolffhardt, stating that he believed an export permit for the collection could be arranged. Nine days later he changed his mind in a further letter. The Property Office did not believe its authority extended to musical instruments and suggested Dr Wolffhardt should consult Dr von Both, Minister for Bohemia and Moravia.

By now Wolffhardt, still at Grundlsee, had decided to take a leaf out of Hitler's book. He declared his patience was exhausted, travelled to Prague and saw Dr von Both on 3 November.

The two men spent hours exhaustively examining the collection. They decided that only 109 out of more than a thousand items were Bohemian in origin and they should remain in Prague, the rest going to Linz. Wolffhardt was not losing a great deal but he was far from happy. He had discovered that plans were being drawn up to move the entire collection to a new building, which seemed to indicate that the Czechs weren't prepared to yield without a fight. Wolffhardt's pessimism was reinforced when he met Professor Werner, chief expert of the Lobkowitz collection, who frostily complained of German looting, mentioning specifically the historic armour collections seized by Ruprecht and the stealing of 'The Hay Harvest' by Breughel, amongst other paintings. Werner added that if this went on, Prague would be reduced from a great European capital to the status of a German village.

Full of forebodings, Wolffhardt made transport arrangements for the collection and gloomily returned to Grundlsee. Three days later he sent a formal request to Prague that the collection be transferred to form part of the Linz library. This had been agreed in Prague but now Dr van Both was anxious to change his mind. He did not need great intelligence to see that a total German defeat was only a matter of months away despite desperate Nazi propaganda to the contrary, and von Both was not anxious to be involved in further plundering at this late stage of the game. He now prevaricated, telling Wolffhardt that it still must go through 'the official channels'. Wolffhardt controlled his patience, still believing that the authority of the Fuehrer mattered as it had in the past.

While he was in Prague Wolffhardt had appointed his own representative, a man called Walter Hoeckner. On 1 February 1945 Hoeckner arrived at Grundlsee with bad news. He told Wolffhardt that after making careful inquiries, he was convinced that not even the first step to hand over the music collection had been taken by von Both's ministry.

Wolffhardt decided it was time for desperate measures. He sent a full report of the situation to Bormann, adding that if there was further delay his transportation plans would be wrecked as he was planning to store the Lobkowitz collection with other Linz items at the Hohenfurth monastery, now a main Linz storage-depot because it was beyond the reach of Allied bombers. Wolffhardt accused von Both's Ministry of deliberately sabotaging the transfer and repeated his generous willingness to forego the hundred-odd items proven to be of Bohemian origin. Cataloguing the remaining nine hundred would keep him fairly busy.

Ten days later he received a reply from Dr von Hummel, successor to Dr Hanssen as Bormann's secretary. It was a copy of an order sent in the Fuehrer's name to Wolf, Director of the Cultural-Political Department of von Both's ministry in Prague, ordering him to expedite the matter without further delay. When a week passed without news, Wolffhardt sent his own letter to Wolf, demanding when he would be receiving the collection. When still no answer came, he sent a telegram of complaint to Bormann, again attacking the stubbornness of the ministry in Prague. In a letter he wrote to Hoeckner Wolffhardt plaintively complained that 'from the German point of view he could not make any sense of the proceedings'. He didn't fully realize that the German point of view was about to disappear altogether.

Wolffhardt was forty-six, young enough still to fight for his country in those desperate last days. Only a few days before his last report to Bormann he had been alerted for military service because things were reaching a critical phase in directions other than the Lobkowitz music collection. On 6 March he was conscripted and vanished into the Army, being succeeded at Grundlsee by Frau Gertrud Laurin, a librarian from Graz whom he had trained to take over from him.

The next day—the first on which she was in sole charge—Frau Laurin received a peremptory note from von Hummel, demanding an up-to-date report on the situation. She hastily contacted Prague and was able to inform him on 9 March that Deputy Reich Protector Karl Frank had intervened. He had declared that Wolf had no authority to act in the matter, but he was personally discussing it with von Both. Whatever was discussed between the two men, Frank was also reading what was now writ very large on the wall. Taking his courage in his hands, he announced that the Lobkowitz collection would remain in Prague and declared that, if this decision was challenged, he was ready to appeal to the Fuehrer himself. No doubt he was fully aware that Hitler had wandered far beyond the sane appeal of any man.

Frau Laurin busily conveyed this news to Bormann, who immediately ordered Frank to hand over the collection to Hoeckner at once and help him to move it out of Prague. Von Hummel sent a copy of this order to Frau Laurin with the request that he be informed immediately by telephone or telegram if any further difficulties arose. The Nazi Empire might be tottering to destruction but the Fuehrer was going to have those musical instruments to play him into Valhalla.

Though in army uniform and under army discipline, Wolff-hardt refused to remain silent. Seven days after his conscription he wrote to von Hummel, asking that everything be done to obtain the Lobkowitz music collection. On 26 March he also received a copy of the peremptory order to Frank to hand over the collection or else. But Wolffhardt found little comfort in it. Even he was beginning to feel that orders from the Nazi hierarchy were now no more than straws in the whirlwind that was being reaped.

At Grundlsee Frau Laurin waited patiently for news, torn with indecision, unable to make up her mind whether to worry the Fuehrer again or not. The days passed and she did nothing. Finally the silence was broken by a telegram sent to her on 19 April by Walter Hoeckner. It stated that von Both's Ministry had finally decided that any attempt to move the collection was far too dangerous because of the rapidly advancing Russian troops. For reasons of safety, it had been moved to a deep shelter in Prague.

It was the final victorious pretext. Every Nazi decision in Prague had been tremendously influenced by pressure from the Czechs. Time had been played out successfully. It was a major victory to offset six years of ruthless pillaging of Czechoslo-vakia's cultural and historical treasures by the barbarians.

*

Poland's collapse in September 1939 saw the Nazis abandon all attempts at legality. Looting was done openly, without concealment behind smooth words. Drunk with the success of their seventeen-day campaign, the conquerors descended on towns and cities like locusts, untroubled by law or mercy. Article 56 of the 1907 Hague Convention states:

The property of municipalities, of Church institutions and establishments dedicated to charity and education, arts and sciences, even when belonging to the State, shall be considered as private property. All premeditated seizure of, and destruction or damage to institutions of this character, to historic monuments, works of art and science is forbidden and should be made the subject of legal proceedings.

As far as the Nazis in Poland were concerned, these words had never been written. Their policy was simpler, expressed without so many involved clauses. Everything was available for seizure; nothing was to be left for the Poles, the rightful owners.

The progress of Nazi plundering during the Second World War was ultimately to reveal a dual policy. Eastwards there was utter ruthlessness, brutal seizures, looting carried out nakedly without pretence and, in Russia, the terrifying new elements of desecration and wanton vandalism that, with the gas-chambers, was to drag Europe furthest back into the Dark Ages. Westwards there was plundering, particularly of Jewish property, but Hitler and other top-ranking Nazis were also ready to purchase with money, an act which in itself meant little, but did preserve a veneer of legality over such transactions.

The first orders to seize Poland's art treasures were issued in October 1939. They came from Dr Kajetan Muehlmann, brought to Warsaw specially to organize the looting. Muehlmann had become a party member a few weeks after the Anschluss and now had the rank of Colonel in the S.S. In Poland he set to work with unsurpassed zeal, issuing instructions for the looting of churches, public buildings, museums and private collections. It was only when this plundering was well under way that two decrees were issued by Reich Minister Hans Frank, Governor-General of Poland, giving Muehlmann the necessary authority. The first on 15 November stated: 'All movable and stationary property of the former Polish State will be sequestered for the purpose of securing all manner of public valuables.' The second decree followed on 16 December, extending the first to cover all *objets d'art* in public possession, all private collections which hadn't already been seized, and all ecclesiastical art treasures.

The main repositories for the loot were centred in Warsaw and Cracow. In the capital the National Museum and the Wilanov Palace were used, both in the charge of Muehlmann's half-brother, Josef. The Cracow repositories, one of which was the Jaghellon Library, were run by Bartel and Kuttlich, directors respectively of the Breslau and Tropau museums.

Muehlmann worked with such efficiency that Poland was picked clean within six months. Everything of artistic value was in German hands, haphazardly stored, awaiting inspection by the leading Nazis as their fruits of victory. To mark the occasion, Governor Hans Frank printed a handsome catalogue of the great treasures he could offer the party's leaders. In it he reported:

> In six months it has been possible to collect almost all the art objects in the country with one exception; a series of Flemish tapestries from the Castle of Cracow. According to latest information, they are now in France, so it may be possible to secure them later.

Governor Frank's catalogue listed paintings by the great masters of Germany, Italy, France and Spain; rare illustrated books and woodcuts; the famous Veit Stoss hand-carved altar, created in Nuremberg but long ago bought by the Poles; antique crystal glass and porcelain; tapestries; rare coins and medals; and antique weapons. The vast treasure had been amassed by looting the national museums in Warsaw, Cracow and other large cities, the cathedrals in Warsaw and Lublin, many churches and monasteries, the homes of the Polish nobility, and numerous university libraries.

As befitted the one he represented, Hans Posse was the first vulture on the scene. He arrived in Poland on 25 November 1939, and inspected the huge caches in Warsaw and Cracow. He conferred several times with Kajetan Muehlmann who had been promoted to Under-Secretary of State. Having undertaken the trip on Bormann's express orders, Posse reported to him on 14 December. He described events in Cracow:

> Almost every day waggons arrive, carrying safeguarded art objects from public, clerical and private collections. They are brought to the new building of the Jaghellon Library, which

is suitable for this purpose. By next February they will be properly arranged. They are busy taking photographs of the important art objects which will be submitted to the Fuehrer in photo-albums. . . .

Posse reported that the 'safeguarding' of valuable art property had been in full swing since 6 October and, as far as he could judge, it was nearly complete. The greater part of the work now consisted of salvaging what had been damaged, such as the furniture and interior decorations of the badly bombed Royal Castle in Warsaw. He clearly indicated to Bormann that he was embarrassed by the riches offered to him now that the Nazi conquering juggernaut was under way. Only what he called 'the higher-class works of art' were worthy of adding to the Linz collection, and he proposed to become even more selective in future. Amongst Polish paintings and sculpture he had found little to interest him beyond the Veit Stoss altar, panels by Hans von Kulmbach in the Church of St Mary in Cracow, a small number of paintings in the Warsaw National Museum, and a Raphael, a Rembrandt and a Leonardo da Vinci in the Czartoryski collection. But he did admire greatly Polish silver and gold handiwork, tapestries, armour, china and bronzes.

Posse hadn't entirely forgotten his first love—the Dresden Art Gallery. He proposed to Bormann that all the salvaged wainscoting, doors, inlaid floors, sculpture, mirrors, chandeliers, and pieces of furniture and chinaware from the Warsaw Royal Castle should be transported to Dresden to decorate the Zwinger Palace. In accordance with Nazi philosophy, Posse justified this action on the grounds that the Royal Palace had been 'completed and furnished by Saxon architects'.

Increasingly the Nazis were delving back into history to lay precarious claims to works of art. No excuse was too slight or too ridiculous to be used. In Vienna they had looted the coronation regalia of the Holy Roman Empire from the Imperial Treasure Room which dated back to the tenth century and included the jewelled crown of the Emperor Conrad, known as the 'Crown of Charlemagne', a shield, two swords and an orb. These had been held in Vienna since 1804 but the Nazis dug up a fifteenth-century decree by the Emperor Sigismund that they should be kept in Nuremberg and promptly shifted them there.

In Poland the same tactics were applied to the Veit Stoss altar, which Posse had decided he did not want. The King of Poland had commissioned Veit Stoss in 1477 to carve this massive work and though it took him ten years, he was well paid for his labours. Now the Nazis claimed that because Veit Stoss was a native of Nuremberg, the altar rightfully belonged to the city of his birth. They brutally pulled it out of the Church of St Mary and carted it away. This great work of art, one of the few in Poland for which the Nazis manufactured an excuse to justify their looting, ended up in an underground bunker opposite the Albrecht Duerer house in Nuremberg, totally dismantled, the twelve ornate side panels, the great central panel, the ten-feet high gilded figures of hollow wood and the statues and pinnacles surrounding the framework all stripped from it, stored haphazardly amidst drab concrete surroundings and suffering total neglect.

While he was in Warsaw Posse learned how nearly the Germans had lost the greater part of Poland's art treasures. Fearing a German invasion, the Poles had started in the previous June to pack into cases the entire contents of the state museums. By the end of July they were ready to be transported but no safe haven for them was offered to this tortured country. The little that was moved eastwards fell into the hands of the advancing Russians.

His tour of inspection completed and his selections made, Posse returned to Dresden, but other Linz agents also made the journey to Warsaw. Dworschak came to examine the confiscated armour and Ruprecht the rare coins. Neither found much to interest him but orders were given to shift many Polish art treasures to Berlin where they were either stored in the Deutsche Bank or distributed amongst the other Nazi leaders.

Posse had asked for three paintings from the Czartoryski collection to be reserved for Linz but through some breakdown of administration, he never received them. For a time they were kept in the Kaiser Friedrich Museum in Berlin before finding their way into the Bavarian home of Governor Frank. During his sojourn in Poland Frank had proved himself no mean looter. He plundered many Polish homes for paintings, tapestries, and dinnerware to furnish his two private residences—the castles at Cracow and Kressendorf. Frank announced that such priceless treasures were safer under his eagle eye, but never announced who was the enemy threatening them.

Hitler received one outstanding gift from Poland—a collection of thirty Duerer drawings, two from the Czartoryski collection and the other twenty-eight from the Lubomirski collection in Lvov. Muehlmann had sent them to Goering, who decided that the time was diplomatic for making a handsome present to his Fuehrer. He personally handed them over and Hitler liked them so much that he kept them at his headquarters for the rest of the war, never being explicit as to whether they would be added to the Linz collection or not.

Of all the countries overrun by Hitler, Poland was to make one of the smallest contributions to the Linz collection. But this was no reflection on her cultural riches. Hitler had made it clear to Posse that he expected and wanted little out of Poland. He was uninterested because his vision of Linz was as the artistic Mecca of Western Europe. The East he dismissed with contempt. He was waiting impatiently for the day when his tanks would sweep through the fields of France to the gates of Paris.

Hitler speaks from the balcony of the Town Hall in Linz in 1938 standing above a multitude of arms uplifted in the Nazi salute. Four-fifths of the population were there to welcome him

Part of the great crowd of townspeople who turned out to give a hero's welcome to Hitler on his victorious return to the town where he spent his youth

A church in ruins, drawn by Adolf Hitler in December 1914,
foreshadowed the ruins he was to create all over Europe

Another Hitler sketch, revealing his talents as a draughtsman. Drawn
while he was a serving soldier in Flanders in the summer of 1917

Adolf Hitler at a
Munich sculpture
exhibition held in
1939. With him is
Heinrich Hoffmann
(*left*), his official
photographer and
one-time art adviser

Panoramic view of Linz, the stuffy provincial town that Hitler planned to transform into the cultural centre of the New Europe

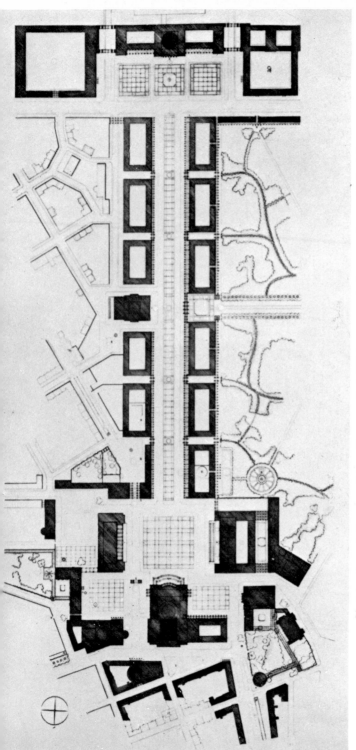

Sketch plan of the new Linz, the so-called 'Hitlerzentrum', from a plan published in Munich in 1944. The cultural buildings were all to be placed along the Prachtstrasse, which ran from the Opera House facing the main square to the railway station on the far right

Dr Hans Posse, Director of the Dresden State Gallery, who created the Sonderauftrag Linz and dominated it until his death in 1942

The coronation regalia of Charlemagne and successive emperors, including the crown, sceptre and orb. Found by the Nazis in Vienna and confiscated on the flimsiest historical pretext

Rubens' 'Ganymede carried off by an Eagle', kept in the Schwarzenberg Palace in Vienna and seized by Hitler. In exchange he gave to the city a collection of porcelain

Baron Louis von Rothschild, the richest man in Austria, whose vast collection of works of art was seized by the Nazis. He was held by the Gestapo for a year until a colossal ransom had been paid

The priceless Czernin
Vermeer, purchased
by Hitler for a
ridiculously low sum,
backed by threats. It was
found at the end of the
war hidden away in the
Alt Aussee salt-mine

Hradčany Castle, Prague,
where Hitler spent his
first night on Czecho-
slovakian soil, 15 March,
1938. He left next
morning with a number
of stolen tapestries

The glorious Veit Stoss altar from the Church of St Mary in Cracow. Commissioned by the King of Poland and carved between 1477 and 1487, it was confiscated by the Nazis because Veit Stoss was a German from Nuremberg

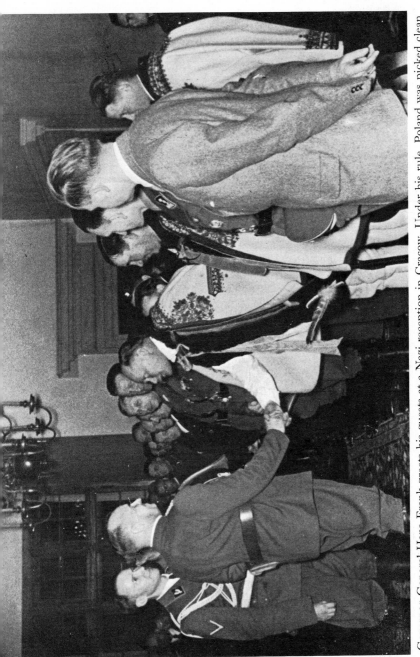

Governor-General Hans Frank greets his guests at a Nazi reception in Cracow. Under his rule, Poland was picked clean of her art treasures within six months

Breughel's 'The Hay Harvest', part of the Lobkowitz collection in Prague, seized by Dr Posse and entered as Item 2124 in the Linz archives

Detail from the famous Hohenfurth altarpiece from Czechoslovakia confiscated by the Nazis in April 1941 and subsequently seized by Hitler for his Linz collection

The Castle Square, Warsaw, with the Royal Castle (*right*), which was ruthlessly looted by the Nazis and most of its interior decorations badly damaged

Castle Square on Liberation Day—17 January, 1945. The Polish flag flies proudly from the pedestal of the destroyed monument to King Sigismund III

The moment of looting. In France a masterpiece by Tintoretto is inspected by a Nazi officer before shipment to Germany, where Hitler always had first choice of the spoils

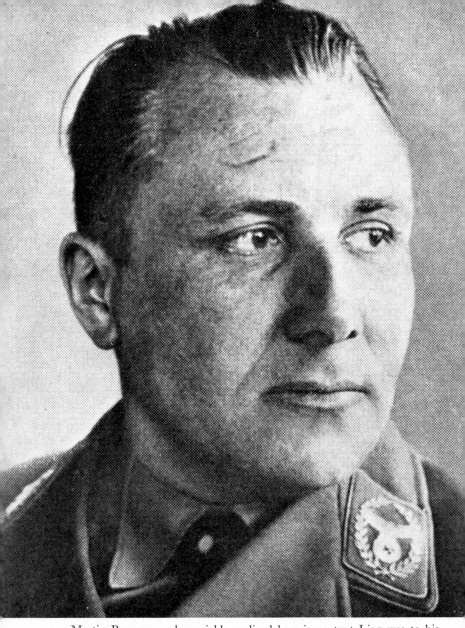

Martin Bormann, who quickly realized how important Linz was to his
Fuehrer, and devoted himself to administering its every detail

CHAPTER FOUR

The Duel with Hermann Goering

As he gazed across a defeated Paris, knowing that the artistic capital of Europe was in his hands, Hitler must have felt that his dream of a greater Linz glorifying his memory was close to realization. Everywhere his armies were victorious and now they stood on the verge of greater conquests. He alone had planned and carried out a great revolution from its very beginnings, transforming a bankrupt country into a world empire. He had commanded history as no man had ever done before. He was confident now that he could fulfil his National Socialist destiny of utterly destroying Bolshevism. In that high noon of ecstasy before things started going wrong, he felt that no matter how grandiose his plans for Linz became, they could never, even so, do his memory justice.

The conquest of Paris offered him unparalleled opportunities for further plundering. Yet he recognized the need to proceed with caution. Because of his policy towards Vichy and the need to persuade the French people to accept their subjugation, even if they weren't prepared to co-operate in building up the New Europe, the seizure of art treasures was confined mainly to the great Jewish collections. But there were always purchases to be made with unlimited supplies of unbacked paper money, reinforced by threats to unwilling sellers.

The promise that Paris offered to Linz, however, was never

fulfilled. Hitler obtained a large number of works of art from the city but the great masterpieces, which Linz had to have if it was to be as Hitler planned, somehow eluded him, even though he repeatedly asserted his right to first choice of everything in a series of decrees. He was frustrated not so much by patriotic Frenchmen, though tribute must be paid to the amazing Rose Valland and others like her, but by a German who was also a leading Nazi—the jovial Hermann Goering, the man on the spot who used the Einsatzstab Rosenberg as his personal instrument, employed to outwit his Fuehrer. Through his native cunning Goering made sure that many priceless masterpieces ended up in his beloved Karinhall where he could enjoy their imperishable beauty instead of being stored away in the Fuehrerbau's air-raid shelters as just other Linz items. It is significant that Hans Posse never dared openly to challenge the fat Reich Marshal's mastery of Parisian treasures. Though he travelled tirelessly throughout occupied Europe, Posse never once visited Paris, preferring instead to issue instructions from a distance to his agents in the city.

The first step to organize an efficient plunder machine under the direction of the notorious Alfred Rosenberg was taken by Hitler as early as 29 January 1940, when the people of Britain believed that the phoney war would go on for ever. By then determined on the conquest of Europe, Hitler concealed his intentions by announcing that he was setting up a research centre that became known as the 'Hohe Schule', though he gave it the grandiose title of 'The Centre for National Socialism, Ideological and Educational Research'. In German it sounded even more impressive.

Its main purpose was to be a cultural Fifth Column. The Nazis had not been slow to learn the lessons of Vienna where, though the people had willingly handed over their country, there was great difficulty in locating some of the art treasures known to be in the city. Before war broke out instructions had been given to German agents in Paris and other European capitals to collect all the information they could about the location of art treasures, particularly in regard to those great collections earmarked for confiscation. With the usual Germanic thoroughness, data was collected on a vast quantity of paintings, sculpture, tapestries, furniture, enamels, gold and silver. In some cases these agents were able to reveal the hiding-places that would be used if the need arose. All this information was passed to the 'Hohe Schule'.

France's dramatic crumbling into defeat, surpassing even Hitler's wildest hopes, found the Einsatzstab Rosenberg still unprepared to start operations. Until it was, the first essential was to freeze the movement of works of art. On 30 June 1940, Field-Marshal Wilhelm Keitel, Commander-in-Chief of the German Armed Forces, issued this decree to General von Bockelberg, Governor of Paris:

> The Fuehrer, on receiving the report of the Reich Minister of Foreign Affairs, has issued an order to safeguard for the time being objects of art belonging to the French State and also such works of art and antiquity which constitute private property. Especially Jewish property is to be taken into custody by the occupational powers against removal or concealment after having been labelled with the names of their present owners. There is no question of expropriation but certainly of a transfer into our custody to serve as a pawn in the peace negotiations.

Similar tissues of lies were issued in Holland, Belgium, and Luxembourg. Until the machinery for plundering was ready, the aim was to lull the occupied peoples into a false sense of security. Great works of art were not being looted, only temporarily taken into custody so as to be used in the game of power politics.

However, there was no need for delay or prevarication in regard to the great Jewish collections. What complaints could the French or Belgians or Dutch have when the Germans had already treated their own Jews far worse? In Paris the task of carrying out these initial confiscations was given to a German Embassy adviser named Baron von Kunsberg, aided and abetted the Gestapo. His powers were announced on 17 July by the German Ambassador Abetz, and his organization, known as the 'Kolonne Kunsberg', was staffed from within the Embassy.

Twelve days earlier Keitel had drawn up a blue-print for the systematic looting of the occupied countries, its outline already suggested to Hitler by Alfred Rosenberg and given the Fuehrer's approval. It authorized the searching of all state archives and libraries, churches and masonic lodges. As with the decree of 30 June, it covered France and the Benelux countries.

The German net around the great art collections was tightened even further by another Keitel decree of 15 July. It was long, detailed and left no loopholes.

Section 1 stated: 'Moveable works of art will not be taken from the place where they are at present or modified in any way whatsoever without the written authority of a commander of the military organization.'

Section 3 stated: 'Moveable works of art whose value exceeds 100,000 francs must be declared by their owners or custodians in writing prior to 15 August 1940 to the competent field commander or some other authority so indicated.'

By these means, Hitler was ensuring that the vast amount of valuable information collected by German agents did not become out of date before the Einsatzstab Rosenberg was ready to operate. Savage punishments were promised to anyone who ignored or disobeyed the 15 July decree.

In his brief two months of glory, von Kunsberg had no shortage of obvious targets. The great Jewish art collections in Paris were among the finest in the world. They belonged to such men as the Rothschilds, Lévy de Benzion, Kahn, the Seligmann brothers who were famous as art dealers, and David-Weill, owner of a magnificent gold and silver collection. As in Vienna, the Rothschilds were pre-eminent, but this time the names were Baron Edouard, Baron Robert, and Baron Philippe. The immense art collections belonging to the family had a total value running into millions of pounds, and some of them did elude Hitler's clutches. A number of paintings were moved in time into the neutral embassies, including the Spanish and Argentinian, where they remained safely throughout the war. Other precious works of art were got out of France in time, travelling in made-to-measure portable cases which the Rothschilds, always realistic about the world's upheavals, had had ready since the Paris Commune of 1873. A few priceless pieces were hidden in a secret room behind a bookcase in the Roth-schild mansion at 23 Avenue de Marigny, which became the home of the Luftwaffe Commandant in France. Often Goering would pace up and down only a few feet away, particularly when he was losing planes by the hundreds in the Battle of Britain, but he never discovered what lay behind the bookcase.

The Rothschilds had hoped to protect their collections by giving them to the Louvre, thus making them national property. Hitler circumvented this manœuvre by ordering Keitel to issue a special directive stating that all transfers of ownership to the French State after 1 September 1939 were 'irrelevant and in-valid'. The decree cited specifically the possessions of the Rothschild family.

Dispersal was also attempted by the family. Baron Edouard hid most of his collection at his farm at Haras de Meautry in Normandy. Baron Robert transported his valuable art treasures from his chateau near Chantilly to Marmande in south-west France. Both these and other Rothschild hiding-places were discovered, the family being far too prominent to escape detection. Before many months had passed nearly four thousand works of art belonging to the Rothschilds had been seized by the Nazis and a large proportion of them were grabbed by Hitler for his Linz collections. They ranged from paintings by Rubens to delicate eighteenth-century snuff-boxes. Trainloads of these and the artistic possessions of the other great Jewish families started to roll into Germany, part of the fruits of victory. Few were distributed amongst the lesser Nazis until Hitler had decided whether he wanted to claim possession through his Linz experts.

By September 1940 Alfred Rosenberg had decided that his Einsatzstab was ready for action. On 17 September Keitel sent this order to the Chief of the German High Command in Occupied France:

Reichsleiter Rosenberg has received clear instructions governing the right of seizure from the Fuehrer personally.

He is entitled to transport to Germany cultural goods which he deems valuable and to safeguard them there. The Fuehrer has reserved for himself the decision as to their further disposition.

Rosenberg, the son of an Esthonian shoemaker who had become ideological leader of the German people, chose as his Paris headquarters the small Musée du Jeu de Paume in a corner of the Tuileries Gardens, near the Place de la Concorde. It was here that his agents brought their plunder for a large staff, mostly Germans, to check, catalogue and label before shipping them to Germany. Looted treasures poured into the building in a fantastic and never-ending stream. In his first two months since taking over from von Kunsberg, Rosenberg handled a total of 21,903 works of art, valued conservatively at well over 500 million reichsmarks.

The Jeu de Paume was more than just a clearing-house. It also served as an exhibition centre, holding private displays of the most valuable plunder which were attended by the top-flight Nazis who sauntered around, selecting whatever they fancied as long as they did not infringe the order of preference laid down from on high. Ironically this order was drawn up by Goering himself in a directive dated 5 November 1940. It gave first preference to Hitler, second to the Reich Marshal for completing his collection, third to the Einsatzstab for distributing amongst other Nazi leaders, and fourth to the German museums. If anything was left over, it was either given to one of the Paris museums or auctioned off to the private art dealers who clustered in Paris, seeking their fat commissions from avid customers in Germany willing to buy almost anything.

Once he had drawn up this order of preference, Goering did everything in his power to ensure that the positions of himself and Hitler were reversed when any great masterpiece became available. He ran very little risk. Hitler stayed in Germany, totally absorbed in planning the invasion of Russia and bolstering up Mussolini, and Posse continued to stay away rather than risk open battle with such a powerful figure in the Nazi hierarchy. Goering was greatly helped by having his own agent on the spot, the clever and loquacious Walter Hofer from Berlin, one of the finest art experts in Germany though still a comparatively young man. Goering also appointed a young art historian named Dr Bruno Lohse as his permanent representative, wangling him into Paris by the simple expedient of putting him in the Luftwaffe with the unobtrusive rank of leading aircraftman.

Unlike Hitler, Goering had a passion for works of art. He wanted to see them constantly. He was also ready to take endless trouble to possess what he wanted. In the thirteen months from November 1940 he visited the Jeu de Paume museum on six different occasions, tearing himself away from his Luftwaffe duties, usually arriving in civilian clothes and staying for several absorbed hours. He was attracted by the element of surprise that was like a lucky dip. On any visit he might come across a great work of art that had only just been seized, delivered a few hours before by one of the many vans constantly drawing up outside the museum. If he was as fortunate as that, the painting went to Karinhall without even being entered in the Einsatzstab's records.

Corruption was rife amongst Rosenberg's employees. Many top Nazis were prepared to give heavy bribes to get something they particularly wanted. But money seldom measured against the power and influence that the gregarious Goering could and did wield to the full. Flattery from the gorgeously uniformed Reich Marshal was flattery indeed. He set about winning the entire Einsatzstab to his side simply by writing fulsome letters of praise to Rosenberg on the excellence of his organization and protecting it from the criticisms voiced in certain quarters of the Wehrmacht. He always defended any member of the Einsatzstab accused of privately lining his pockets, even when the allegations were true. The only way Goering failed as a protector was in not detecting Rose Valland, a courageous Frenchwoman who by ingratiating herself became a trusted member of the Einsatzstab's staff. By day she sabotaged the work by such intentional errors as wrongly labelling crates. By night she would remove negatives, have them printed and returned next morning, thus compiling a secret file, complete with biographical data and photographs, of the German personnel employed in the museum.

Detached as he was in his Eagle's Nest, Hitler wasn't entirely ignorant of Goering's rivalry, which the latter frankly admitted at the Nuremberg trials. If he could not accuse him, Hitler could still take precautions. On the advice of both Posse and Heinrich Hoffmann, he told Goering that he must see a photograph of every work of art before it left the Jeu de Paume museum. Only when he had examined them and made his selection would Goering be able to exercise his prerogative. Where the system was fallible was Hitler's inability to ensure that every masterpiece which fell into the hands of the Einsatzstab was photographed and the prints sent to him. Quietly Goering was able to suppress this process, particularly when it came to his own special preference for paintings by Rubens and the Dutch school of the seventeenth century. Thus many paintings which should have had 'A.H.' chalked on their frames left the Jeu de Paume museum marked 'H.G.' instead.

Goering's belief that the Einsatzstab Rosenberg, set up though it was by Hitler, was his own personal looting organization, its main task the satisfying of his great passion for priceless masterpieces, was typically illustrated by events that occurred early in February 1941. Goering was not so foolish as to fail to send Hitler a large number of photographs of works of art seized by the Einsatzstab for not even he could conceal the staggering number of confiscations that had been carried out. On 4 February he went to a meeting at the Quai d'Orsay, attended also by a Rosenberg field commander named von Behr. The Reich Marshal took him on one side and handed him a sheaf of photographs, indicating which were Hitler's selections and which were his own. Needless to add, Goering had chosen the best of everything.

The next afternoon at three o'clock Goering arrived at the Jeu de Paume museum personally to supervise the packing of the paintings, furniture, Gobelins tapestries and valuable ornaments. He issued orders for the entire contents of the museum, mainly comprising parts of the collections of the Rothschilds and Seligmann brothers, to be dispatched at once to

Germany. There was sufficient to fill twenty-five express baggage cars and the only exceptions were those works of art selected by Hitler and himself which were to be loaded on two railway trucks and attached to a special train taking Goering back to Germany the following week.

While all this activity was proceeding, Goering was taken on one side by an art expert named Dr Bunjes, who expressed his concern at the recent protests emanating from the French Government at Vichy. It had described the activities of the Einsatzstab as being 'in defiance of the Hague Convention'. Goering told him firmly: 'It is my orders you have to follow.' But Bunjes was persistent, forecasting that further stronger protests were certain to be made. At this, Goering put his arm avuncularly round Bunjes's shoulders and replied: 'Dear Bunjes, let me worry about it. I am the highest justice in the land.' It was what he sincerely believed as far as this museum and Paris was concerned. Like the Reich Marshal, Bunjes was to commit suicide soon after the end of the war—but for different reasons and in different circumstances.

Goering travelled on his special train the following week. It stopped at the rail terminus of Neuschwanstein, south of Munich. The two railway trucks were unloaded while Goering reported their safe arrival to Hitler. Those pieces earmarked for the Fuehrer were stored in the Fuehrerbau in Munich while Goering moved on with his share of the booty, personally making sure that it safely reached Karinhall. Like Hitler, he had dreams, albeit more modest, of glorifying his memory by building an art museum. It was to be on his estate in the forest of Schorfheide and, though smaller than Linz, Goering believed its contents would be in far better taste. He had already decided when he would present the museum to the Greater Reich—12 January 1953, on his sixtieth birthday.

The Nazi leaders have often been accurately described as gangsters. By 1940–41 they were at the height of their power. Most of Europe had been conquered and, wrapped as they were in the trimmings of state, holding great office, wearing gorgeous uniforms bespattered with decorations, they may have deluded themselves into believing that they were the new race of supermen. The fact remains that they were predatory hooligans, terrorizing a continent instead of a city. Their basic qualities were rarely so frankly revealed as in an amazing letter sent by Goering to Rosenberg on 21 November 1940 in which he displays greed, boastfulness, arrogance, cupidity, cruelty and a willingness to lay hands on any base weapon that might serve his purpose.

Goering sent the letter for what he called 'personal information so that no false ideas can occur'. He started by saying that he specially welcomed the setting up of the Einsatzstab, then quickly asserted his prior rights over the other Nazi leaders who were also casting avid eyes towards the rich loot in Paris.

> I must point out [he wrote] that other authorities also claim to possess powers from the Fuehrer. First of all the Reich Foreign Minister [von Ribbentrop] who several months ago sent a circular to all authorities, claiming amongst other things, power for the occupied territories and stating that the safeguarding of art treasures was his responsibility. Moreover, the Reich Propaganda Minister [Goebbels] is still delegated, I believe, to determine the date relevant to the cultural goods which were stolen from Germany and which should now be returned. . . .

The picture emerges. These were not the men to run the New Europe but savage boars circling the same trough. Then Goering offered his blatant bribe.

> I have promised to support energetically the work of your staff and to place at its disposal that what it could not hitherto obtain, namely transportation and guard personnel, and the Luftwaffe is assigned to give the utmost assistance.

This was the total misuse of men in uniform, an action that would have appalled the old-type German general with his sense of honour. Goering went on boastfully:

> I should like to call your attention to the fact that I have

been able to obtain especially valuable cultural goods from Jewish owners. I obtained them from hiding-places that were very difficult to find. I discovered these a long time ago by means of bribery and the employment of French detectives and criminal agents. This activity continues as does the activity of my foreign exchange investigating authorities in scrutinizing bank vaults. . . .

By the last Goering was making it clear that not even the sanctity of the bank vault was to be observed by the Nazis. All safe deposits that aroused suspicion were being searched. One example of many occurred on 26 September 1941 when a Monsieur Braumuller entered the Société Générale at Avachon, armed with an authority to investigate the vaults issued by the Einsatzstab Rosenberg. He removed two cases packed with paintings and deposited in the name 'M. Phillippe de Rothschild'.

In his letter to Rosenberg, Goering made it abundantly clear what he wanted. 'I already possess today through purchase and barter perhaps the most important private collection in Germany, if not in Europe.' He itemized it—the early German masters, the early Dutch and Flemish, the work of the French Gothic artists (paintings, as well as sculptures), an extensive and highly valuable collection of seventeenth-century Dutch paintings, a small but good collection of eighteenth-century French, and a number of works by Italian masters. He described his plans for one day donating this great collection to the Reich, adding: 'The Fuehrer has welcomed my plan, as well as supported it.'

But great as it was, Goering confessed that it was not complete. For that he needed what he called 'a few pieces from the Jewish cultural goods', adding hurriedly: 'I shall submit things from time to time to the Fuehrer.' He told Rosenberg that what he wanted was 'a very small percentage of the hundreds and thousands of paintings but I consider this percentage all the more justified in that, through my efforts, which can be proved, I brought in a very large part of the art treasures'.

Goering got what he wanted. He and Rosenberg struck up a working relationship against Hitler which ultimately led to their both being discredited within the party at the same time. But while they both flourished, Goering was able to send to Karinhall such paintings as a Venus by Boucher, 'Atalanta and Meleager' by Rubens, 'Adam and Eve in Paradise' by Teniers and another Venus by Lucas Cranach the Elder, whom Goering particularly admired. All these Hitler would have certainly wanted for Linz—if he could have found out that they had been confiscated.

Wisely Goering did not overplay his hand. With thousands of works of art being seized by Rosenberg, there was much that Hitler coveted and received. On 5 February 1941 a typical selection was made for his Linz collection and sent to Neuschwanstein three days later. It consisted of forty great paintings, including a Rembrandt, two Goyas, Vermeer's 'The Astronomer', a Frans Hals, two Watteaus, three Bouchers, two Fragonards, Gainsborough's 'Portrait of Lady Hibbert', and a Ter Borch. Thirty-four of these paintings had belonged to various members of the Rothschild family.

When the paintings were examined at the Fuehrerbau after delivery, two of the Bouchers were found to be missing. Over his signature, von Behr, Rosenberg's Chief of Staff in Paris, had scribbled the words: 'Could not be loaded.' The two missing paintings finally turned up in Munich on 20 March and nine months later the entire consignment was sent to Kremsmuenster because of Allied air attacks. The sole exception was Boucher's large portrait of Madame de Pompadour, which remained in Munich until the end of the war.

Goering's influence over the Einsatzstab Rosenberg was so complete that Dr Robert Scholz, head of its Pictorial Arts Section, found the courage to question in writing whether confiscated items should be sent to the Fuehrer. He wrote to Bormann on 11 December 1940 asking if it was correct that the Sonderauftrag Linz had some authority over the Einsatzstab. Shocked by such audacity, Bormann sent him a sharp reply, ordering him to contact immediately Dr Hans Posse, whom he described as 'the plenipotentiary of the Fuehrer', and reminding Scholz of the decree of 5 November which had been drawn up by Goering himself.

Bormann sent a copy of this letter to Posse, with a covering note stating:

> Obviously Dr. Scholz was not aware that
> 1) even without the intervention of any civilian German offices, all art treasures in occupied territories come under the Fuehrer's right of disposition, and
> 2) that the administration on behalf of the Fuehrer is in your hands.

To make sure that there would be no further 'misunderstandings', Bormann wrote again to Posse in Dresden on 31 December. He informed him curtly:

> The Fuehrer desires that the paintings and furniture in Paris be brought to the Fuehrerbau, Munich. I request that you give Scholz the necessary directions.

Posse did as he was ordered, but as he was still reluctant to go to Paris and personally cross swords with Goering, even direct orders from Hitler had no effect on the Reich Marshal's subsequent conduct. Gripped by his collector's passion, Goering did not care how much Hitler glowered from afar.

Posse grew increasingly unhappy over his inability to control events in Paris. His authority as the Fuehrer's representative was being deliberately flouted, an authority clearly laid down in a directive sent from Berlin by Dr Lammers, to all commanders of the occupied territories. Lammers told them:

> After Austria's union with the German Reich, when the property of the enemies of the State was seized and confiscated on a large scale, the Fuehrer, in order to prevent any possible abuse from the very outset, reserved for himself the right of disposition of seized and confiscated art objects, particularly those of extreme value.
> It has now been suggested to the Fuehrer that a comparable reservation be made to territories occupied by German troops. The Fuehrer has approved the suggestion, reserving

for himself the decision as to the disposition of art objects which have been or will be confiscated by the German occupying authorities. It is irrelevant whether local authorities have also effected seizure. German measures will take precedence on all accounts. The Fuehrer's appointee for the disposition of the art objects is the Director of the Dresden State Art Gallery, Dr Posse.

Informing you hereof, I request you to provide within your sphere of action that Dr Posse be notified in the event that art objects are confiscated by German authorities.

But Posse was not being notified by the Einsatzstab Rosenberg. Paris was flooded with German art dealers and agents, many of whom, particularly Karl Haberstock and Frau Maria Dietrich of Munich, were to make fortunes out of selling paintings to Hitler for his Linz collections. Now they were only too eager to inform Posse of Goering's powerful influence over the Einsatzstab and how great paintings were being seized and then mysteriously vanishing. Their reports did nothing to diminish Posse's unhappiness.

In March 1941 an account of 500,000 reichsmarks was opened for his use in the Reichskreditbank in Paris but Posse was well aware that money was not the answer. Barely a month later he wrote to Bormann, expressing his doubts and demanding a clear statement of his authority. Bormann replied with the suggestion that Posse review all the confiscated works of art held at the Schloss Neuschwanstein, the chief repository of the Einzsatzstab, when an inventory then under way had been completed. He could then requisition anything he thought worthy to be put aside for Linz. But it was a half-hearted proposal, Bormann being certain without possessing proof that great paintings had gone from Paris to Karinhall without ever being catalogued at Neuschwanstein. Not even he was prepared to suggest that Posse visited Karinhall, examine Goering's collection and choose what he wanted in the name of the Fuehrer.

Posse was not alone in his reluctance to throw the gauntlet down to Goering. Dr Leopold Ruprecht, in charge of the Linz armour collection, and Dr Franz Dworschak, in charge of the coin collection, both visited Paris on a number of occasions as members of a committee devoted to 'the recovery of works of art stolen by the French from Germany since 1794'. Neither visited the Jeu de Paume museum or made any contact with the Einsatzstab Rosenberg.

The conflict between Hitler and Goering was essentially one of quality rather than quantity. In the long term the power remained with Hitler and later measures by Bormann, when Rosenberg was being rapidly discredited within the party, were to make sure that the Einsatzstab's accumulated twenty thousand works of art were to remain intact, with Hitler's right to first preference when the war was finally won firmly established. But Hitler's vision of Linz was that its museums should contain only the greatest works of art, and much of what was stored at Neuschwanstein and other repositories was unworthy of being included. It was Goering who had seized the great masterpieces which would certainly have been chosen for Linz. In this respect, his opposition was most effective and bitterly resented by Dr Posse, the man responsible for placing Linz at the pinnacle of European art.

Goering's efforts apart, the rich field tilled by the Einsatzstab in Paris was such that it still became the greatest source of works of art for Linz. It operated so ruthlessly and effectively that the total collection it gathered in was greater than any possessed by the British Museum in London, the Metropolitan Museum in New York, the Louvre in Paris or the Tretiakov Gallery in Moscow.

CHAPTER FIVE

A Clear Field in Holland

In Holland there was no one of the stature of a Hermann Goering to challenge Hitler as plunderer-in-chief. In the art market of The Hague, where prices rapidly soared skywards as the victorious Nazis furiously bid against each other for valuable works of art they could take home to their wives, the Fuehrer's authority still went unchallenged and Hans Posse was able to bring off some of his greatest coups on his master's behalf.

Holland surrendered to the German Army on 15 May 1940, finding itself ruled by Reich Commissar Seyss-Inquart, who had not forgotten Dr Kajetan Muehlmann, his protégé from the Viennese days, and was well aware of the latter's success in gathering in Poland's art treasures. One of Seyss-Inquart's first moves in his new office was to bring his protégé to The Hague to conquer fresh fields. Such was German efficiency, Muehlmann arrived on 16 May, the day after the surrender, and within a matter of days was confiscating, purchasing, and 'safeguarding' works of art on a large scale. At the same time he was well aware that he could not proceed with the same ruthlessness he had exhibited in Poland.

Unlike Rosenberg, Muehlmann was fully conscious of the advantages to be gained from ingratiating himself with the Fuehrer and sensible of the authority possessed by Hans Posse.

After ensuring that his organization, the 'Dienststelle Muehl-mann', was firmly established, he travelled to Berlin early in June. From there he telephoned Posse in Dresden to inform him that the time was opportune to make large-scale purchases for Linz from Dutch art dealers and private collectors. He suggested that this could be done with German reichsmarks, thus avoiding the complications that would ensue in obtaining large amounts in a foreign currency. And he added that though he was charging a ten to fifteen per cent commission on confiscated works sold at auction to cover his organization's expenses, he was willing to waive this in regard to any work of art purchased for the Fuehrer's Linz collection.

Smarting with resentment over the way Goering and Rosenberg were working against him in Paris, Posse was only too eager to fall in with Muehlmann's proposals. On 10 June he wrote to Bormann, reporting the conversation and suggesting that he waste no time in travelling to The Hague. Posse added:

Even though a large part of the Dutch art trade's important works are likely to have been moved to America before the outbreak of war, I believe that the trade will still contain enough objects desirable for the Fuehrer's collection.

Events were not to prove him wrong. Three days later Bormann replied, stating that the Fuehrer approved of Dr Posse's going to Holland but he was only to purchase works of art of the highest class. With so many countries now occupied, Hitler was also raising his sights.

Posse arrived in The Hague exactly two months after the first German troops had crossed the border. He found himself an office and adopted the title 'Referent fuer Sonderfragen' ('Adviser on Special Questions'). He found the art market temporarily exhausted as the defeated Dutch had handsomely cashed in on the high prices their victors were prepared to pay. Large numbers of paintings had changed hands in such rapid succession by the time of Posse's arrival that many important Dutch dealers and collectors had called a halt and were not selling to anyone.

Posse's first move was to seek the assistance of middlemen, the most important being a counsellor of the legation named Wickel. He reported to Bormann by letter that 'unfortunately recent mass purchases in Holland have driven prices very high' and enclosed what he described as 'a short secret report by a Dutchman who is friendly to the Germans'. It stated:

> The present situation is as follows. One of several groups buy everything they can get hold of. Prices don't matter. The dealers invest their working capital in paintings and rugs already in Holland, as they cannot import anything. Private people buy to invest their money. For that reason there must be one of several groups of speculators. They buy at any price, hoping with the help of their connections in Berlin to make huge profits. They hardly expect to find a better customer than Germany. It reminds some of them of the best times with the Americans.
>
> A big collection of paintings will come into German hands. But then Germany will have to pay ten times as much for it as one would normally pay because of having to buy with the speed demanded. The big Jewish dealers will take the profit.

Bormann took the broad hint. By arrangement with the Reich Commissar for the Occupied Netherlands, a special account was opened in The Hague in the name of Dr Posse. Unlike the one in Paris, there was no mention of a limit of 500,000 reichsmarks. In such financial matters Hitler was unconcerned, as he could always print more money if he needed it.

From the beginning, Posse had the active support of the Nazi authorities in the Netherlands. Bormann had written to both Seyss-Inquart and Schmidt-Munster, ordering them to give every assistance to Dr Posse, who possessed the Fuehrer's direct authority. As his chief buyer, Posse appointed Dr Erhard Goepel, a thirty-year-old art expert who travelled frequently to Paris, making purchases for Linz in both capitals. In Holland Goepel employed as his chief adviser a Russian-Jewish dealer named Vitale Bloch. Goepel had protected

Bloch from the anti-Jewish laws in exchange for having first refusal of any art treasure Bloch discovered to be up for sale. Highly regarded as a connoisseur, Bloch also bid at auctions on Goepel's behalf.

Aided as he was by the full co-operation of the Dienststelle Muehlmann, Posse was able to send his first purchases to Munich in December 1940. They totalled twenty-seven paintings and Posse could be proud of every one of them. Among them were Pieter Breughel's 'Carrying of the Cross', two portraits by Rubens, Gerard Dou's 'Portrait of Rembrandt's Father', Canaletto's 'View of San Marco, Venice', a Rembrandt self-portrait, Rubens's 'Christ Taken Prisoner', Jan Steen's 'Village Marriage', and Jacob van Ruisdael's 'View of Haarlem'.

Eight months later the industrious Dr Posse was able to ship a further fifty-three paintings, comprising mainly works by Dutch and Flemish artists of the seventeenth century. They included Gerard Ter Borch, Adriaen Brouwer, Jan Breughel, Jan van de Capelle, Joos van Cleeve, Jan van Goyen, Wilhelm Kaaf, Pieter Lasterman, Jan Steen, Fritz Snyders, and Willem van de Velde. Hitler was highly delighted with both consignments and Posse basked in the glory heaped upon him. These purchases did much to assuage the bitterness he was feeling about Paris.

To make sure that his part in these successes was not overlooked by the Fuehrer, Muehlmann produced an elaborate photo-album entitled 'Selection of Acquisitions from December 1940 to March 1941: Dienststelle Mühlmann, The Hague'. It contained photographs of the second consignment of paintings, each with a beautifully mounted caption, and was presented to Hitler as a gift from a loyal servant. Later Muehlmann was to regret bitterly that he had indulged in such obsequious flattery for the album was to prove his undoing.

After his capture by the Allies Muehlmann claimed that his Dienststelle had been a legal organization which had fairly purchased every work of art that had passed through its hands. He strenuously denied that he had ever confiscated a single painting. Unfortunately, his presentation album to Hitler was found amongst the Fuehrer's private library buried deep in the Alt Aussee salt-mine. It contained details of ten paintings confiscated from the Franz Lugt collection in The Hague for which Lugt received no payment. Even more damning was the photograph of the painting, 'Mountain Landscape' by Henri met de Bles, which had formed part of the Alfons Jaffe collection. For its caption, Muehlmann had written: 'The Jaffe collection was taken from Berlin about four years ago, part to London and part to Holland. The Jewish owner is in London. The part remaining in Holland was in the Leyden Museum and was confiscated (*beschlagnahmt*) by us.' In face of this evidence Muehlmann ceased his denials.

There can be little doubt that Posse spent more of Hitler's money in Holland than in any other of the occupied countries. Prices were extremely high but generally unimportant to a man busily engaged in building himself a world empire. Early in October 1940 Posse was granted an interview by Hitler in order to discuss the purchase of two collections. Bormann was not present and later Posse wrote him an account of the meeting:

We did not talk about special matters. I merely showed the Fuehrer photos of the latest purchases, and reported about the future purchases of some objects and certain whole collections. For instance, that of Otto Lanz of Amsterdam—at present on exhibition in the Rijksmuseum—and that of Franz Koenigs, one of the most famous collections of old master drawings in Rotterdam, containing 24 drawings by Duerer, 40 by Rembrandt and so on. I have been interested in it for several months.

In principle, the Fuehrer agreed to the acquisitions. The price for the part of the Koenigs collection now on sale is 1,500,000 gulden; for the Lanz collection (Italian paintings, Renaissance furniture, sculpture, *objets d'art*) more than 1,000,000 florins. I have suggested the choice of objects more suitable for the Fuehrer's purpose, which justify their price, and that the extensive remainder be put up for auction where we shall surely be very well repaid. I shall be travelling this week to France to attend to certain matters, and I am going

from there via Brussels to The Hague to take up transactions which have fallen due meantime, especially the Koenigs collection. I wish to arrive earlier than certain other
people, and catch them napping. . . .

The Koenigs collection was one of the few occasions on which
Goering appeared on the Dutch scene as a rival to Hitler.
Through his agent, Miedl, he had already bought nineteen
paintings belonging to Franz Koenigs, an Amsterdam banker
who was killed in a railway accident at Cologne in 1941. But in
The Hague Goering did not possess the influence he exercised
in Paris and Posse was given the double satisfaction of outwitting the Reich Marshal and obtaining a collection of old-
master drawings that he had coveted so much.

The purchase of the Otto Lanz collection proved to be far
more difficult, involving considerable haggling and drawn-out
negotiations. Lanz was a former consul to Switzerland whose
widow had had the good sense to stay on in Switzerland but had
given her permission for her late husband's collection to be
loaned for exhibition at the Rijksmuseum. Walter Hofer was the
first on the scene, but reported to Goering that it was mostly
second-rate items trying to appear as first-rate. Posse came next
and did not agree, somewhat influenced by the collection containing important specimens of Italian art which could only
rarely be imported from Italy. Posse decided the collection was
worth buying.

On 24 January 1941 he informed Bormann of the progress of
the negotiations. The Lanz family was asking for 2,900,000
Swiss francs plus a further 250,000 Dutch gulden. After
assurances from Dr Lammers that payment could be made in
these currencies, Posse offered 2,000,000 Swiss francs plus the
quarter of a million gulden. But the Lanz family weren't
satisfied and demanded that the price be raised. In Posse's
absence, negotiations were carried out by Wickel, the legation
counsellor, and the haggling went back and forth until it was
finally agreed to add a further 100,000 gulden to the original
offer. In addition Posse would also pay the commission due to
the Dutch agent involved in the transaction.

Posse wrote:

I am of the opinion that in consideration of the great
artistic value and rarity of the objects in the Lanz collection,
the limit of counter-offer has been reached. I also believe that
a purchase under these circumstances is extremely favour-
able and I, therefore, ask permission to purchase this collection which, in spite of many weaknesses, contains so many
important works of art. . . .

He did not have to wait long for an answer, despite the huge
sum involved. Three days later Schmidt-Munster of the Nazi
administration in The Hague was writing to Bormann:

In accordance with yesterday's telegram from Obersalzberg, I hereby confirm that counsellor of the legation Wickel
has been informed by me and that he will close the contract
to purchase. . . .

Permission to export the collection into Germany was
arranged by 26 February. Exchange difficulties held up payment
to Madame Lanz but on 19 March she received the two million
Swiss francs after the Swiss Government had first refused to
credit the money to her account as it came from a Berlin bank.
On 28 March Posse was able to write to Bormann that the last
arrangement had been finally completed, making the sale
effective. On 15 April he and the Lanz collection left Holland
en route for Munich, where Hitler's latest prize was presented
to him.

*

Though he had been extremely successful in making the
acquisitions he wanted in Holland, Posse was not entirely
happy. He had received a serious setback in regard to the large
'Venus' by Hans Baldung, the early sixteenth-century German
painter who exhibited a sensual delight in portraying the nude
female figure. Posse had come across it in the Kroeller-Mueller
Museum at Otterloo and voiced his enthusiasm in a letter sent

74

to Bormann on 23 September 1940. But for once Goering, who had seemed satisfied to confine himself to dominating the Einsatzstab Rosenberg in Paris, bestirred himself. His agent in The Hague reported on the Baldung and Goering acted immediately, demanding that Muehlmann authorize a forced exchange on the museum—the 'Venus' for a number of modern French paintings that Goering despised. Unaware that Posse was interested, Muehlmann yielded to Goering's pressure. By the time Posse had received the go-ahead from Bormann, the painting was firmly in Goering's hands.

But Posse had learned to forget past disappointments. He was far more concerned over the high prices he was being forced to pay. Too many German buyers were competing for too few masterpieces and values were reaching astronomical heights. In one letter to Bormann Posse suggested that either private purchases by German dealers be prohibited or prices be limited to 1,000 or 2,000 florins per item. He added:

When one realizes that according to the recently received lists of purchases, they now amount to eight million Dutch gulden up to the end of 1940, it is regrettable that prices for pictures in Holland have been raised by the competition of the many German buyers, who appear more and more in Holland.

But this appeal was not favourably received by Bormann, who was well aware how successful the Fuehrer had been in making purchases on the free, if somewhat inflated, Dutch market. In Posse's report dated a month earlier—15 January 1941—he had stated that one-fifth of all the paintings exported from Holland into Germany were going to the Linz collection. Despite the competition, in the seven months May to December 1940 Posse had spent 1,500,000 gulden plus a further 1,400,000 gulden for the Koenigs collection. In addition, a further 250,000 gulden had been spent in the first half of January 1941 and there was no sign that the flow of money was easing.

Posse had also informed Bormann that Goering had spent

1,500,000 gulden in Holland but few of his purchases were great masterpieces as he exercised little influence over the Dienststelle Muehlmann. On the remaining purchases made up to the end of 1940, five million gulden had been spent by German dealers. In a number of instances Heinrich Hoffmann was the middleman and later he ensured that the paintings were offered to Hitler for his Linz collection.

One month later Posse was admitting that his estimate of eight million gulden spent up to the end of 1940 was a conservative one. Many purchases had been made but not paid for, others were still going through the clearing-houses. He told Bormann: 'One would not exaggerate in saying that the total up to the end of 1940 is fifteen million gulden, perhaps even more.' Most of these purchases had been freely entered into, the collaborationists in Holland eagerly seeking out Posse and other Linz agents, anxious to curry favour with the all-powerful Fuehrer. Other Dutch art dealers, though far from being pro-Nazi, took the view that the war was lost and there was no reason why they shouldn't make huge profits if the Germans were willing to pay inflated prices. Now the fighting, as it was, was over, business was business. In those early months of total defeat it seemed that nothing could ever loosen the Nazi grip on Western Europe.

Late in January 1941 Posse made another killing. At the Weinmueller auction-house he outbid all other dealers for the best of the substantial collection owned by Goudstikker, a famous Amsterdam art dealer. He reported to Bormann:

In accordance with your request, I have inspected the picture collection at Weinmueller's. They are mostly well-known old Dutch things from the art dealer Goudstikker and the rest of the pictures which Lange in Berlin could not sell, what many people call 'the rubbish of the Netherlands'. There were only a very few acceptable pictures. I was able to obtain the best things, namely, six pictures for a total of 54,000 reichsmarks, including a magnificent, even if polished-up, portrait by Paolo Veronese, a Verspronck, Parmigianino, Palamedes, Nicolaes Maes, and a Guercino.

76

Posse later bought two other pictures as well and the eight paintings were sent to Munich as one consignment, Reger entering them as Items 1403 to 1410. Previously Hitler had obtained eight other Goudstikker paintings, bought from Frau Maria Dietrich. These included a Gerard Ter Borch and a Claes Molenaer. In addition, he visited the storage depot kept by the Berlin art dealer, Meidl, just behind the Reich Chancellery and inspected a large number of other paintings once owned by Goudstikker. He chose sixteen altogether and must have been pleased with his purchases as they included Rembrandt's 'Music Lesson', Teniers' 'Soldiers at the Inn', Jan Steen's 'Quack', a seascape by Willem van de Velde, and a tavern scene by Adriaen Brouwer.

Hitler also paid 40,000 reichsmarks for Isenbrandt's 'Madonna and Child', 35,000 reichsmarks for a portrait by the fifteenth-century German painter, Elsner, 17,500 reichsmarks for 'Hercules and the Lion' by Lucas Cranach the Elder, and 8,000 reichsmarks for Jan van Goyen's 'Carts on the Dunes'. Through Goepel he bought directly from Holland a baptismal scene by Bloemart and Castiglione's 'The Animals Entering Noah's Ark'.

His haul from Holland had been substantial. Whatever Linz was to lack, it would not be works by the great Dutch and Flemish masters.

*

Hitler had invariably covered his art dealings in Holland with a veneer of legality as part of his policy not to antagonize the occupied countries while German divisions were engaged elsewhere. Pressure might be brought to bear but money did change hands, even if it wasn't always a fair price. But in one important instance Hitler was to countenance the use of overt brutal threats. The stake was not only one of the most important private collections in Europe but also Hitler's own desire to wreak a final vengeance on a man he had hated even before he had become Chancellor of the Reich in 1933.

His name was Fritz Mannheimer and he was born in Stuttgart in 1891. Three other facts need to be stated about him. He was a financial genius. He was a Jew. He hated the Nazis, not only because of their persecution of his people, but because he loved Western civilization deeply.

Mannheimer learned his banking in the German Reichsbank in Berlin. By the age of twenty-eight he had become a figure of prominence and wealth amidst the economic chaos of a defeated post-war Germany. He speculated brilliantly as inflation made the mark almost worthless and became one of the new millionaires. He was extremely fat, weighing over eighteen stone, but behind the plump, smiling features lay a keen brain that measured everything with a slide-rule's precision. In those early days Mannheimer was an economic pirate, out for personal gain, but amassing money did not blind him to the political situation. He saw that inevitably Hitler would gain power and what that would mean to himself as a Jew. He decided it was time to quit Germany before it was too late.

He went to Amsterdam and joined the old-established banking firm of Mendelssohn and Co., one of the strongest private banks in Europe. It wasn't long before Mannheimer dominated the firm but money was no longer his chief interest. He wanted to use his talents to shore up Europe's crumbling resistance to the totalitarian régimes, and Mendelssohn's became the accredited bankers of the Weimar Republic. Even so, like a reflex action he could not control, Mannheimer still made money and by the mid-1930s he was said to be worth at least £10,000,000, possibly double that amount. Translated into present-day purchasing power, it was a colossal fortune.

Like the Rothschilds, Mannheimer bought works of art not only as investments but because he enjoyed living amidst great beauty. He crammed his mansion in Amsterdam's aristocratic Hobbemastraat with paintings, antique silver, gold and crystal, and Gobelins tapestries. He owned works by Rembrandt, Vermeer, Fragonard, Watteau, Carlo Crivelli, Chardin, Guardi, Canaletto and many others. He possessed a discerning taste and though he paid high prices, they were never foolish. As his collection grew, the mansion in Hobbemastraat became no longer large enough to hold it. At Vaucresson near Paris Mannheimer bought the Chateau Monte Christo and filled that also with great art treasures. Yet all this time, even as he acquired great wealth and possessions, he did not forget the persecution of the Jews, or that his beloved Western civilization was in danger of being obliterated by the brutalities of National Socialism. Mannheimer had long hated Hitler and what he stood for. He decided to fight him with the two weapons he possessed— money and his genius as a financier.

Mannheimer decided that France could be the only strong bulwark against the onrush of Naziism. He decided to devote himself to trying to help her put her economic affairs in order. He formed a syndicate of Dutch and Swiss banks which undertook the responsibility of a number of short-term French Government issues. The newspapers christened them 'golden bullets' and privately Mannheimer contributed several million francs to France's national defence programme.

The activities placed him high on the Nazi list of archenemies. The Dutch Nazi Party shrieked vituperation at him but otherwise was ineffectual, Mannheimer being too powerful and the Mendelssohn bank too long established. But outside Holland the threats against him increased as Nazi power grew after the successes in the Rhineland, Austria and Czechslovakia. They took the form of exerting pressure on banks not to accept Mendelssohn bills since bankers, like most other people, were learning to jump through Hitler's hoop when he barked at them.

Mannheimer had little inkling of what was going on. But even if he had known all the facts, it is doubtful if he would have stopped what he was doing. He suffered from an extremely weak heart and the doctors had told him he would not make old bones. He decided that while there was life in him, he would enjoy both the luxury of possessing great wealth and fighting wholeheartedly something he hated without reservation or scruple.

In June 1939, when he was forty-eight, Mannheimer secretly married an attractive 26-year-old Brazilian girl, Mademoiselle Marie-Antoinette-Jeanne Reiss. The ceremony was performed at the village church at Vaucresson and after the honeymoon, Mannheimer returned to Amsterdam, his wife staying on at the

Chateau Monte Christo. At this time Mendelssohn and Co. were backing even more French short-term issues than usual. They had sold well in Switzerland but growing Nazi influence in Holland had caused them to fail. Mannheimer still had to meet payment to the French Government which caused him to be temporarily short of liquid funds. Normally a bank with as strong a reputation as that possessed by Mendelssohn's would have met the situation with the minimum amount of aid—which would have been readily forthcoming. In the financial world it helps no one when a long-established bank fails. But wherever Mannheimer turned, there was no offered help. The Nazis had at last succeeded in cutting every life-line.

On 9 August Mannheimer took a mysterious telephone call in his office. He told no one the identity of the caller but immediately left Amsterdam for Vaucresson, where he had a long discussion with his wife. Later that day he died in her arms, the official pronouncement of a heart-attack never completely killing the rumours of suicide. Mannheimer was buried in the village churchyard after a funeral service had been held in the church where he had walked as a bridegroom two months earlier. The day after his death all payments were stopped by Mendelssohn and Co. The bank's assets were put at £24,400,000, its liabilities at just over £25,000,000, a deficit of £650,000. Not an over-large sum in this world of high finance but sufficient to declare the bank bankrupt, putting in the creditors and freezing Mannheimer's personal fortune.

It was hastening what would have inevitably happened nine months later. In 1940, just before France fell, Mannheimer's widow moved most of the art treasures from the Chateau Monte Christo to Vichy, leaving only a few items at Vaucresson. The rest of the large collection stayed in Amsterdam. After his troops had swept through Holland, Hitler decided that he alone would inherit the numerous paintings and other works of art so lovingly collected by a man he had hated so greatly. But the situation was complicated as there could be no confiscation on the simple grounds that it was Jewish property. Mannheimer's collection was now owned by his creditors, most of whom were not Jewish.

Hitler made his first move on 4 February 1941. Bormann sent a letter marked: 'Very urgent. To be delivered immediately to General Commissar Schmidt in The Hague.' It was so urgent that it bore not only the date but the actual time of writing—20.40 hours. Bormann wrote:

Please inform immediately Dr Posse, who is at present in Holland, that the Fuehrer wishes the immediate purchase of the Mannheimer collection. This collection should be bought at once by the Fuehrer's orders.

I request the Reich Commissar to refuse permission to purchase to all other services, but to support the sale to Dr Posse.

Previous to this letter enormous pressure had been brought on the Mannheimer creditors to sell the collection. After months of negotiations and meetings, they had finally agreed, but the price they were asking was steep. Seven and a half million gulden, equal to 225 million francs. Now by issuing this order through Bormann, Hitler had at one stroke eliminated all competition. If the collection was to be sold, there would be only one buyer to bid for it.

Posse decided to leave the negotiations to the ever-willing Reich Commissar Seyss-Inquart, aided by his art expert, Dr Kajetan Muehlmann. Seyss-Inquart was more than usually eager to do his Fuehrer a favour because he had particular reason to ingratiate himself with Hitler. At that time he was using money belonging to the Reich Commissariat to finance his stock-market operations, which were bringing him a large fortune. He was buying dollar bonds of German external loans on the Dutch market and selling them to the Deutsche Golddiskontbank, a branch of the Deutsche Reichsbank especially entrusted with operations in foreign exchange. With this money he was buying U.S. bonds whose nominal value was three times as much and hoped to sell them after the war at an enormous profit. Seyss-Inquart was well aware that he might be called to account for manipulating the Reich's money at any time and Hitler's goodwill would then be invaluable. As it was, the first official objections from Berlin did not come until the middle of 1944.

Muehlmann was instructed to open negotiations with the Mendelssohn creditors and use brute force from the outset. He made an offer of 5,500,000 gulden for the large part of the Mannheimer collection still in Amsterdam—a price far below its value at prevalent market prices—and added the threat that if it was not accepted, every work belonging to the traitorous Fritz Mannheimer would be confiscated as enemy property. The creditors sought other buyers, found no one ready to bid for so many highly prized masterpieces, and became convinced that these were no idle threats. Faced with no alternative, they accepted the offer.

To show how highly he regarded his Fuehrer, Seyss-Inquart paid for the collection out of a special fund of his Reich Commissariat. Over the years he intended to earn this money and a great deal more from his stock-exchange manipulations. If he could show he had spent such a large sum on such a generous gift to Linz, it would be a powerful argument for Hitler supporting him in the event of trouble with Reich accounting officials.

As he had done for Governor Hans Frank in Poland after stripping that country clean, Muehlmann produced a sumptuous three-volume catalogue of the Mannheimer collection, printed in Vienna and bound in pigskin. Probably the most important single item in the Dutch section was Rembrandt's portrait of the Jewish doctor, Ephraim Bonus, one of the masterpieces of his later period. After the Mendelssohn creditors had been paid, the collection was sent to Munich for cataloguing and then stored at Hohenfurth in Bohemia until deeper penetration by Allied planes caused it to be buried deep in the Alt Aussee salt-mine.

But Hitler was not satisfied. He still did not possess the entire Mannheimer collection, some of the greatest paintings still being in the possession of Madame Mannheimer at Vichy. He was forced to wait three years until the time was ripe to open negotiations to purchase twenty-five canvases, besides various other works of art. Again Muehlmann acted on Hitler's behalf but this time he employed an intermediary to make direct contact with Mannheimer's widow. This was Ferdinand Niedermayer, Administrator of Property seized by the Reich in France with an office at 15 Rue Beaujon in Paris. Haggling started, but before agreement could be reached, the old fox Karl Haberstock in Berlin got wind of what was going on. In April 1944 he wrote to Niedermayer, saying that he wished to make a speedy trip to Paris to discuss the twenty-five paintings that were about to be bought for Linz. If, by chance, some were not wanted, he would like to buy them as a private dealer. Whatever was left over, Haberstock was sure he could make a handsome profit by re-selling them.

Niedermayer promised to find out this information. Just three weeks later he wrote to Haberstock, informing him that the deal had been completed and he had been sent orders by Dr von Hummel, personal secretary to Martin Bormann, that all the paintings from Vichy as well as the few left behind at Vaucresson were to go to Linz. He added: 'I regret that I am not in a position to take your purchasing wishes into consideration.'

The price paid by Hitler for the twenty-five paintings was fifteen million francs. Completion of the deal meant that his wish to possess every piece of the Mannheimer collection had been fulfilled to the letter. It proved to be the third largest collection that Hitler acquired, exceeded only by those of the Rothschilds and the Schloss family.

Out of the twenty-five paintings, the largest price of four million francs was paid for a St Mary Magdalene by Carlo Crivelli which had once hung in the Kaiser Friedrich Museum in Berlin. Next came a painting by the French painter, Fragonard, which fetched two million francs. Another Fragonard was sold for 850,000 francs, four more for 800,000 francs each, and Chardin's 'Soap Bubbles' also realized 800,000 francs. There were also two Watteaus, a Guardi canvas of a Venetian church, and other works by Ingres, Canaletto, van Ruisdael and Molenaer. The paintings were sent direct to Alt Aussee where the rest of the collection was already stored.

Thanks to the efforts that at the last minute averted the blowing-up of the salt-mines, it was possible to return the collection to Holland after the war. In 1950 it was sold at one of the most financially successful auctions ever held in Holland.

CHAPTER SIX

The Fortune-Makers

Because the Nazis were never loth to exchange unbacked paper money for property, including great works of art, money was never of primary importance in the building up of the Linz collections. Every transaction of the Linz agents furthered the deliberate Nazi attempts to undermine the economy of the occupied countries, and such purchases caused far less trouble than outright confiscations. After the war many German art dealers found they could not retain possession of a work of art even though they had paid money for it, had properly completed the transaction and there had been no hint of any element of duress. As for the collaborationist art dealers and collectors, they did not hesitate to sacrifice their country's prosperity and financial stability for immediate personal profits.

Whenever circumstances did not offer sufficient excuse for a forced sale or confiscation, Hitler was content to adopt the normal bartering methods of exchanging his money for goods. To this end, an elaborate organization of agents, dealers, informants and go-betweens was established throughout Europe, backed by a system of travel facilities and financial arrangements. As most of the recognized Linz agents operated solely on a commission basis, they often competed with each other for any painting they knew the Fuehrer would want, forcing prices at auctions up to astronomical levels so that only the richest could compete.

Some dealers cynically paid fantastic prices for paintings by German artists, which they privately believed to be of little value, because they knew they were admired by Hitler and other Nazi leaders. On the other hand, the works of the great Impressionists were ignored and vilified, yet it is those that have greatly increased in value in the post-war years.

Not being the supreme warlord, Goering at times had to exercise great control over both his agents and the prices he paid for paintings. At one auction he instructed Walter Hofer that his maximum bid must be 15,000 reichsmarks. If that sum was passed, he was to drop out. Hofer obeyed and the painting was finally sold for 17,000. But no such paltry considerations ever worried Hitler, particularly when it came to the great masterpieces, recognized as such for centuries throughout the world. Often they were not greatly to Hitler's personal taste but he was prepared to bow to the verdict of history and pay huge prices for them. For two Rembrandts belonging to Etienne Nicolas—a landscape and a portrait of Titus—Hitler agreed to pay three million reichsmarks plus a further 90,000 as commission to the Paris art dealer, Roger Dequoy. The Titus had once hung in the Hermitage at Leningrad and the landscape had formed part of the Stroganoff collection. The deal was originally set up by Haberstock who waived his commission, acting on the principle that he could afford to be generous on major art transactions when he was fleecing Hitler in selling him less important paintings.

Hitler also paid 900,000 reichsmarks for another Rembrandt and 675,000 for Boecklin's 'Italian Villa', an enormous sum for a work by an artist not considered to be in the first-rank.

Purchases for Linz were made inside and outside Germany, mainly through auction-houses or by dealers buying directly or indirectly from private owners. The most important auction-houses were Lange in Berlin, Weinmueller in Munich and Vienna, the Dorotheum in Vienna and the Hotel Drouot in Paris. Hitler also made purchases in the neutral countries, buying six paintings from a Lucerne dealer in May 1941. He paid 89,300 reichsmarks for two Spitzwegs, a Buerkel, a Lenbach, a Boecklin and an Uhde—all artists he greatly admired.

Prominent dealers like Frau Maria Dietrich and Karl Haber-stock sold direct to Hitler and, in turn, they employed agents to act for them at auctions. At the Hotel Drouot Haberstock was represented by Madame Weyll, a friend of Baron von Poellnitz. Theo Hermssen, a Dutch dealer in Paris, acted for Hildebrandt Gurlitt, another prominent German art dealer who operated first from Hamburg before moving to Dresden.

Fully aware of the importance of the professional art dealers if Hitler was to obtain the best of what was being offered for sale, Posse made sure they were given every facility for travelling through the occupied countries. Posse himself had a special travel certificate signed by Bormann which read:

> The Director of the Dresden Painting Gallery, Dr Hans Posse, identified by passport of the Commissioner of Police, No. VI 971/39, has personal orders from the Fuehrer, as I hereby certify for the action of all ministries, to travel to the occupied territories of the Netherlands and Belgium in order to buy works of art for the Fuehrer.
>
> All German ministries of the occupied countries are hereby asked to give Dr Posse every assistance to fulfil the task assigned by the Fuehrer.

Bormann also wrote in the name of the Fuehrer to Gauleiter Muetschmann in Dresden to ensure that a large car was made available at all times for Dr Posse. Posse could also demand air-craft and trains to be laid on specially for him if the need ever arose.

Similar travel certificates were supplied to all accredited Linz agents, stating their connexion with the Linz project and asking for the assistance of all the appropriate Nazi Government agencies. Later this system was much abused, certificates being issued not only to genuine dealers but also to those who had only the flimsiest connexion with Linz. Gustav Rochlitz, the Parisian art dealer, was given a Linz certificate to enable him to keep out of the Army. After receiving it, he sold only four minor paint-ings to Linz. Another dealer, Wolfgang Gurlitt of Berlin, was given a Linz certificate to facilitate a trip to Strasbourg where he had family business to attend to. His only contribution to Linz was a small statue, sold long before he received his certificate.

In purchasing pictures, Posse had the great advantage of having funds readily available in his name in France, Holland and Italy. These were generously replenished whenever he needed more money. Only in 1944 were the strings tightened so that payments for art treasures bought outside Germany became possible only through the clearing-house system. In the final months of the war Bormann even issued orders that no prospective purchase could be made by any Linz agent without the details first being submitted for the Fuehrer's approval. Even Hitler had grown tired of paintings being thrust at him by dealers so confident that the Fuehrer would buy them.

But when Hitler did buy, the dealers had their bills paid by Dr Lammers in Berlin with cheques drawn on the Berlin bank of Delbrueck, Schickler & Co., and transferred through the clearing-house. Commission was never itemized separately, the dealers including it in the price they asked, varying their profit percentages in accordance with how generous they thought the Fuehrer might be. If a graph could be made of Hitler's generosity, it would be shown to be high when France fell and Russia was invaded, but fell steadily downwards from the time of Stalingrad and El Alamein.

When a foreign currency was needed, permits had to go through Bormann's office and invariably it was an elaborate procedure. Various fees had to be paid to government departments and German customs, which, in some cases, totalled sufficient to add another seven per cent to the price of the painting. Export licences also had to be obtained and Haberstock touched on a general complaint which went much deeper than the usual grouse about red tape. Writing from the Hotel Ritz, Paris in October 1941 to Tchernikoff, Director of the Service for Purchases and Sales Abroad, a department within the Nazi Finance Ministry in Paris, Haberstock commented:

German buyers are very much interested in purchasing paintings and works of art, most of which are in the hands of

private persons who do not wish to publicize such sales; not
with any intent to evade French law but simply out of consideration of their official standing in French life . . .

In short, many prominent people, who embraced the reputation of being good patriots, were just as anxious to do business
with the Nazis as the open collaborators. They were attracted
by the high sums that German dealers were willing to pay and
Haberstock did not want to frighten them off. But they were reluctant to sell because they felt that putting the transaction on
record by an export licence application was as good as putting
their heads in a noose. Haberstock was concerned not with their
hides, but that his business should not suffer.

German agents for Linz can be roughly divided into three
categories: Nazi officials who bought works of art to curry favour
with Hitler, dealers and agents within Germany, and dealers and
agents in the occupied countries. The last two overlapped to a
considerable extent and many of these men had strong connexions with the Nazi Party, joining because it made the top-
ranking Nazis potential customers. Once they had been appointed Linz agents, none of them hesitated to use the fact that
they were acting on behalf of the Fuehrer to impress, influence,
browbeat, and terrorize prospective sellers. They arrogantly
flourished their certificates before minor army and party func-
tionaries with outrageous demands for preferential treatment.
Usually they were given it.

*

One man who did not fall precisely into any category, yet
played a considerable part in building up the Linz collections,
was Heinrich Hoffmann, who remained close to Hitler until
1944 when Bormann eased him out of high party circles.
Though Posse's appearance had ended his reign as Hitler's unofficial art adviser, he still retained his influence, based mainly
on the fact that he sincerely shared Hitler's admiration for the
florid and vulgar nineteenth-century German school, unlike the
many dealers who paid lip-service and smiled quietly behind

Hitler's back. With the special status given to him as the official photographer of the Nazi movement, Hoffmann was able to travel freely throughout Germany and the occupied countries. He quarrelled with everyone who knew anything about art— Posse, his successor Hermann Voss, Haberstock and many others, but few were able to curb his activities because Hoffman instinctively knew the paintings Hitler would like. He was thus able to arrange many sales for the Linz collection and rarely incurred Hitler's later disapproval. From the beginning Posse had recognized the danger and had acted the strong man, insisting that he must be solely in charge of Sonderauftrag Linz, and making it clear he would brook no interference from Hoffmann, whom he despised. In this he succeeded, Hoffman retaining no say in policy matters—but he still flourished and was able to put a great deal of money into his own pocket.

Hoffmann liked to be known as 'Professor' but this was purely an honorary title bestowed on him by Hitler in 1937. Because he drank heavily, other art dealers sometimes suggested he should be given the further title of *Reichstrunkenbold* (Reich drunkard). Hoffmann was too confident of his own position to allow such taunts to worry him. He was in direct contact with the Fuehrer, able to have his ear almost whenever he wanted it. He had also introduced Hitler to Eva Braun when she was one of his employees, and was well aware that many would-be sellers did not hesitate to use him as the best avenue for obtaining Hitler's personal consideration of their paintings.

Despite his protestations after the war that he never bought a painting specifically for Linz, the records show that Hoffman was extremely active as a middleman. Writing to Bormann on 15 January 1941, Posse asserted that Hoffman acted as the intermediary for a substantial part of the five million gulden worth of paintings bought up to the end of 1940 by Germans in Holland.

Far more damaging to Hoffman were the meticulous records kept by Hans Reger at the Fuehrerbau in Munich, the clearing-house of nearly everything that was bought for Linz. Born in 1898, Reger was an architect with a minor party position in the city. He was placed in charge of the Linz records in 1938 and maintained them almost until American troops entered Munich in 1945. His work became increasingly responsible as the intake of works of art grew from a trickle into a flood. Possessing a neat, meticulous mind, Reger took a great pride in efficiently recording everything in great detail. Every item was catalogued, photographed and assigned a Linz collection number. Being a painstaking man, Reger also recorded the names of the individual agents who had obtained each work of art, and it was this that was to betray Hoffmann's protestations that his hands were clean as far as art looting was concerned.

According to Reger's records, a total of 155 paintings reached the Fuehrerbau the source of which he could enter as being Professor Heinrich Hoffmann. The first arrived on 3 August 1940 and the last on 4 September 1942. Most of them were by German artists but there were also thirty-six Dutch paintings and two Italian. The last work in his name was the large painting by von Looz-Gorswarem impressively entitled 'Frederick the Great at the Battle of Lethe', which no doubt comforted the Fuehrer as the tide of victory was stemmed in Russia and the Western Desert. Reger entered it as 'purchased by Professor Hoffmann for the Fuehrer'. Others were entered as 'from Professor Hoffmann' or 'from Professor Hoffmann and Dietrich' or 'from the Almas Gallery and Professor Hoffmann', the last two betraying the close business association between Hoffmann and Frau Maria Dietrich, who ran the Almas Gallery in Munich and wisely specialized in nineteenth-century German paintings. Like Hoffmann, she had a keen appreciation of Hitler's personal tastes.

The records do not reveal how much Hoffmann made out of his Linz sales, though the grand total must have been large indeed. One of the few transactions that have come to light show that on 31 January 1941 he paid 29,500 reichsmarks for three paintings which he sold to Hitler three weeks later for 35,000 reichsmarks. Hoffmann was extremely active in Holland where he bought at least thirty paintings through the Dienststelle Muehlmann. He was also permitted to buy confiscated works at knockdown prices, paying only 400 reichsmarks for a landscape by the seventeenth-century Dutch painter, Simon de Vleiger, tantamount to giving it away. He also paid 700 reichsmarks for Brekelenkam's 'Man with a Pipe' and the ridiculous price of 2,000 reichsmarks for a landscape by the great Dutch painter, Willem van de Velde. All these came from the Alfons Jaffe collection. Of all his purchases in Holland, twenty-two were confiscated paintings, nine from the Jaffe collection, and all bought from agencies which dealt solely with confiscated art treasures.

Another full-time Linz official who played a prominent role as a supplier of paintings was Dr Erhard Goepel, who was only thirty when he was appointed chief buyer in Holland, responsible directly to Posse. He was paid a salary as an employee of the German Government of the Netherlands, but travelled freely around Europe from his home in Leipzig.

Goepel made a number of purchases in Paris, including a seascape by van de Velde, 'Interior of a Ruin' by Hubert Robert and a pair of large Panninis, all bought from dealers and re-sold to Hitler. According to Reger's records, Goepel was also the source of a life-size equestrian portrait of the Marquis de Legans from the workshop of Rubens, acquired in Paris and delivered to the Munich gallery of the Brueschwiller brothers where Hitler inspected it. Other Linz paintings obtained through Goepel were a still life by the Flemish painter Franz Snyders, a seascape by the Dutch painter Ludolf Bakhuysen, a still life by Adrianssen, and Batoni's 'A Cardinal'. Even as late as July 1944 Goepel was still an active buyer, purchasing for Linz Bloemart's 'Baptismal Scene' from Count Limburg-Stirium in The Hague. It was dispatched safely to Munich.

Goepel was extremely ambitious. Despite his youth, he had believed he would get Hans Posse's job when it fell vacant but Hermann Voss was preferred instead. Unlike his relationship with Posse, he was never happy working under Voss, mainly because he felt he could do the job so much better himself. His loyalty towards the Sonderauftrag Linz diminished until he started to seek buyers elsewhere. In Paris he bought a van Dyck, a Hobbema and a Rubens which he moved to The Hague. Normally Hitler would have had first refusal, but these three great paintings were never even offered to him. Goepel also found other buyers for a number of nineteenth-century French paintings he was able to purchase.

*

Thanks to the influence of Heinrich Hoffmann, Frau Maria Dietrich of the Almas Gallery in Munich became the most prolific supplier of paintings to Linz. Hitler was her best customer, the source of her great fortune. Totally unknown before the war, she rose to great prominence amongst German art dealers in a matter of a few years. Her daughter, Mimi, was a close friend of Eva Braun, a relationship which drew the mother within the Fuehrer's circle. Frau Dietrich sold him more than 270 paintings, and though only a few were major works, she made up any lack of quality by weight of numbers. She bought paintings on a fantastic scale, often paying grossly inflated prices because she knew very little about art. From Paris alone she bought eighty paintings which she re-sold to Hitler, always at a handsome profit, and these were only a quarter of the paintings she bought in Paris in the period 1940–44. Like some women buy hats or dresses, she went shopping for works of art, always obeying her own limited taste. In the prosperous years during the war her annual income was over 500,000 reichsmarks, compared with the mere 47,000 reichsmarks she earned in 1937. She had amazing energy and vitality, even if it was mostly misdirected. Competition from other dealers at the auction-houses never frightened her. She welcomed it, encouraged it, and waxed very rich despite her foolish errors.

Maria Dietrich was born in Munich on 28 June 1892. At the age of eighteen she gave birth to an illegitimate daughter, christened Mimi, the father being Jewish. In 1921, when the child was ten, she married Ali Almas-Diamant, a Turkish Jew in business in Munich as a tobacconist. She accepted both the Jewish faith and Turkish citizenship, and the marriage was a happy one until the Nazis came to power. Their anti-Semitic policy brought the inevitable strains and stresses, and for four years Frau Dietrich ran into considerable trouble with the authorities until she divorced her husband in 1937. It was the turning-point of her life. When her German citizenship was restored to her in 1940, she was already making a vast fortune from selling paintings to Hitler.

Frau Dietrich set up as an art dealer at 9 Ottostrasse in Munich. Despite her divorce, she retained her husband's name by calling her business 'The Almas Gallery'. Like Heinrich Hoffmann, she greatly admired the nineteenth century German painters and had little time for Renoir, Matisse or Picasso. She worked hard but at first made little headway until Hoffmann heard of her, sought her out and quickly realized the lucrative possibilities that could arise out of an unofficial business partnership with this energetic, single-minded woman. Eva Braun was then working for Hoffmann and struck up a friendship with Frau Dietrich's daughter. Hoffmann wasted no time in introducing Maria Dietrich to Hitler, and in a matter of months she became the Fuehrer's favourite art dealer, even superseding the famous Karl Haberstock. She was one of the few able to sell a painting direct to Hitler without seeking the prior approval of Dr Posse or his successor, Hermann Voss.

Her rise was meteoric. To paraphrase a famous Churchillianism, never before in the field of art was so much money made by one who knew so little. Her income soared from 47,000 reichsmarks in 1937 to 483,000 in 1938. It rose to 570,000 reichsmarks in 1941, maintained that level in 1942, and dropped slightly to 505,000 in 1943. By 1944 the tide of war had turned against the Nazis and the problem of protecting art treasures from Allied air attacks was far more pressing than buying further ones, but in that year Frau Dietrich still managed to earn the substantial sum of 216,000 reichsmarks. Between the years 1940 and 1944 her profits from dealing with the Fuehrer amounted to 616,470 reichsmarks and though he was her best customer, there were many others in a loot-laden Germany where there was fierce competition for any work of art that came up for sale. People were also eager to buy from her for the snob value, being able to boast they had bought from the woman who was selling so many paintings to the Fuehrer.

Like some women competing in a man's world, Frau Dietrich

93

had few scruples. She showed none in trading on her friendship with Hitler by charging him inflated prices which he invariably paid without a murmur of protest. Generally her profit margin on any painting she sold to Hitler was about fifty per cent, sometimes a little less. But in the sale to him of thirty-six paintings her profit in each instance was over 100 per cent, in seven over 200 per cent, and in six others over 300 per cent. It was little wonder she could bid like a madwoman at auctions and be able to absorb the occasional bad buy which not even she could re-sell.

Frau Dietrich bought mainly at the German auction-houses, particularly Lange's in Berlin. Her insatiable buying and unnecessarily high bids rapidly made her notorious. She was given a Linz travel certificate in 1941 but made only one trip to Holland, which she spent visiting friends and not buying anything. Previously she had bought part of the Goudstikker collection through Hoffmann and another dealer, Meidl, and some of these paintings she sold to Hitler.

Her main foreign buying was confined to Paris where she had a number of agents in her employ. These included Thérèse Vatchnadze, a Russian princess, and the dealer, Yves Perdoux. Typical of the hundreds of letters she received was one written by Perdoux from Paris:

Dear Madam,

I thank you for your letter and hope that you like the purchases.

I shall definitely reserve the picture by Scorel [the 16th century Dutch painter] for you though it has been asked for by various parties.

M. Larcade leaves today for Nice. Several offers have been made for the two beautiful 12th century column-statues which I have reserved for you. M. Larcade was told that we had agreed on a price. We are ready to purchase them at any price. M. Larcade does not want to sell any more to anyone except you.

For my part, I have prospects of getting a first-class early portrait by Cranach the Elder and a very beautiful Lucrezia by the same master. I have already reserved two Hubert Robert landscapes.

Please write me when you definitely expect to be here. It is urgent that I talk to you before you to anybody on anything.

Heil Hitler

This letter was dated 29 January 1941, a time when Paris was overflowing with German dealers fighting each other whenever a painting popped to the surface, yet dealers were prepared to reserve works of art for the absent Frau Dietrich, such was the pre-eminence of her position. Some would sell to her and no one else because she was generous and never bilked. They were never informed of the high profit she made in her turn.

Surprisingly one of her strongest allies in Paris was Dr Bruno Lohse, Goering's permanent agent. Though she bought mainly for Hitler and seldom did business with the Reich Marshal, Lohse was willing to help her solely on the basis of friendship. He passed on to her titbits of information that he could not use himself and escorted her round the various galleries in Paris. Through him she bought Bocksberger's 'Creation', which she sold to Hitler, and 'Epiphany' by François Boucher, Madame de Pompadour's favourite painter. She paid 140,000 reichsmarks for it and promptly charged Hitler 180,000.

She had much more trouble with four small landscapes in oils by the eighteenth-century Venetian painter, Francesco Guardi. She bought them and two works by Pannini for a total of 60,000 reichsmarks. When she offered them to Hitler, he refused to buy them after being advised by Voss that they were fakes. Never daunted, the irrepressible Frau Dietrich got all her money back by selling the Guardis to a Berlin architect named Nadolle, who gave her to understand that he was acting for the party labour leader, Robert Ley. Thus the money she got for the two Panninis was all profit.

In Paris she made many big purchases. At the Loebl gallery she bought Winterhalter's famous portrait of the Duchess de Morny, later destroyed during an air-raid on Munich. At the same gallery she acquired 'Romantic Landscape' by Caspar

David Friedrich, one of the better of the nineteenth-century German romantic painters whose Wagnerian vision of Nature was much admired by Hitler. At the Mandl gallery she bought an extremely large canvas called 'Harbour Scene', painted by the French Impressionist, Eugène Boudin, who had such a decisive influence on Monet.

In the period 1940–44 more than a hundred French dealers and private owners, most of them in Paris, sold works of art to Frau Dietrich. They were paid promptly and she seldom haggled about the price. Though most of what she bought went to Hitler, she numbered nearly all the top Nazi leaders amongst her clientele. She also found the German State itself a good customer, selling more than twenty paintings through Bormann for hanging in the Berlin Reich Chancellery. She kept meticulous records, never tried to conceal her ledgers or keep false sets, and only on one occasion was there proof that she had traded in a confiscated work of art. This was 'View of Honfleur' by the French Impressionist, Camille Pissarro, who was a disciple of Corot. With the assistance of Bruno Lohse, she obtained the painting from the Einsatzstab Rosenberg by exchanging it for two small Portuguese fifteenth-century panels which she had had some difficulty in selling. The Pissarro had once formed part of a private Jewish collection in Paris seized by Rosenberg, and as Pissarro himself was a Jew, Frau Dietrich decided it would be unwise to carry it on her books and transferred the ownership to her daughter, Mimi. Despite her great wealth and established position, her memories of once being the target of Nazi anti-Jewish laws were still painfully alive.

Judged solely as an art dealer, Maria Dietrich was one of the most honest in Germany. She brought to this cut-throat trade an air of innocence that never deserted her. Amazingly she prospered despite being duped on so many occasions. Various confidence-tricksters could have rarely found such a fat bird so easy to pluck, and her ledgers were full of entries which read: 'Marked down because false'. Perhaps a more sensitive person would have taken these humiliations to heart and given up, but Frau Dietrich sailed calmly on, a massive Bruennhilde sublimely self-confident and totally ignorant of her ignorance. Her saving grace was that Hitler was likewise, though there were the odd occasions when even he rebelled, once going as far as to rebuke her in writing. It happened in May 1942 when she sent him a watercolour which she claimed was the work of Rudolf Alt. It must have been an extremely clumsy fake because even Hitler was able to spot it. On his instructions, Bormann wrote tartly to her:

The so-called Alt watercolour, which you enclosed with your letter of 2. 5. 42, I have shown to the Fuehrer. Both he and I consider it an obvious forgery. If possible, this affair should be investigated without delay so that the perpetrators can be punished.

This shows once again how important it is in the future to study very carefully old paintings.

The words 'very carefully' were heavily underlined to emphasis the Fuehrer's displeasure but Bormann might as well have saved himself the trouble. Nothing could change Maria Dietrich. She went on her way incapable of being reformed, still committing the most glaring errors of judgement. On one occasion even an expert of the stature of Hans Posse faltered when he bought from her a painting after Frau Dietrich had assured him that it was by François Boucher. Posse was influenced because he greatly admired Boucher and was determined to obtain as many as possible of his paintings for the Linz collection. Later he discovered it was a fake and an angry exchange of letters ensued over a period of many weeks, finally resulting in Frau Dietrich offering him by way of recompense a Rubens sketch and a portrait by Jan van Scorel, both of which she had bought from the Weber collection in Hamburg. Yet if she prevaricated, it was not because she wished to evade her moral responsibility in the matter. The letters went on for weeks because it took Posse all that time to convince her the Boucher was a fake when she had been utterly convinced otherwise.

When she was in Munich, Frau Dietrich did sometimes consult an art expert. He was Dr Ernst Buchner, Director of the Bavarian State Museum. But he lost patience with her after she had shown him numerous second-rate and fake pictures, and once turned her out of his office from sheer exasperation. Though Hitler bought a huge number of paintings from her, probably only a few would have formed part of the final Linz collection for hanging in the projected Fuehrermuseum.

*

The only comparable rival to Maria Dietrich as a seller to Linz was Karl Haberstock. When war broke out, he was sixty-one years old, one of the most prominent art dealers in Germany and a member of the Nazi Party since spring 1933. Once he had played the role of kingmaker in Posse's appointment he made the latter feel that every painting he bought from Karl Haberstock was also the payment of a further instalment off a debt. Haberstock had three fat years in which he sold over a hundred paintings to Hitler, thirty-six of them entered in Reger's records as being delivered to the Munich Fuehrerbau on 2 April 1941. But, as so often happens, Posse's successor, Hermann Voss, wanted nothing to do with his predecessor's favourite. He disliked and distrusted Haberstock, who sold nothing to Linz after March 1943 when Voss was appointed.

Haberstock stuck to his policy of waiving his profits on the major pictures when he could make so much money on the minor deals with no questions ever being asked. Besides forgoing his commission on the two Etienne Nicolas Rembrandts for which Hitler paid three million reichsmarks, Haberstock claimed he received not a penny when he helped Hitler to buy the Mendelssohn Rembrandt for 900,000 reichsmarks and Boecklin's 'Italian Villa' which had belonged to the Duke of Eldenburg, for 675,000. For his part in the purchase of Watteau's masterpiece 'La Danse' for 900,000 reichsmarks, Hitler gave him some furniture to show his appreciation but no cash.

As far as Hitler was concerned, Haberstock had several years' start over all other dealers and only Maria Dietrich was to overtake him. In 1937 he bought Spitzweg's 'The Serenade' from a Bohemian collection in the Prague National Museum and sold it to Hitler for 50,000 reichsmarks. Hitler liked it so much that he hung it in his office in the Fuehrerbau. In 1938 Haberstock bought Makart's 'Triumph of Beauty' from a Polish collector and Hitler paid him 20,250 reichsmarks for it. By using an account he held in the Swiss Bank in Regent Street, he bought a number of paintings in London which went to the Fuehrer. He acquired Van Dyck's 'Jupiter and Antiope' for £3,000 and Hitler paid him £3,600 for it. He also bought a Rubens, a Canaletto and a Palma Vecchio, all of which went to Hitler.

After the fall of France, Haberstock centred most of his activities on Paris. He had no difficulty in obtaining complete freedom to travel where he wished, and made a number of visits to the French capital, always staying at the Hotel Ritz and always announcing his arrival in the *Gazette des Beaux-Arts.* Throughout Parisian art circles he distributed special announcement cards reading:

> Mr Karl Haberstock sends his most cordial greetings and begs to inform you that he is in Paris at the Hotel Ritz, Place Vendôme (Opera 2930). He invites you to offer him first-class pictures by old masters.

Compared with Maria Dietrich's total of a hundred French dealers and private collectors willing to do business with her, Haberstock's total was seventy-five. But unlike her, his knowledge of art was profound after a lifetime of buying and selling; he bought with care and circumspection, and a much higher proportion of his purchases were masterpieces. He was rarely snubbed but he did receive the cold-shoulder treatment from the Duveen brothers, whose gallery was in the Place du Marché St Honoré. They answered a letter from Haberstock by firmly declining to see him and all his subsequent efforts to transact business with their gallery failed.

Haberstock was totally unscrupulous in his business methods and busily cultivated the French collaborationists, both in Paris and Vichy France. The most important of these was Roger Dequoy, the business partner of Georges Wildenstein who became owner of the firm when it was 'Aryanized' in May 1941 through Haberstock's influence. Like Posse, Dequoy found himself firmly in Haberstock's debt but it was one he willingly discharged. He sold Haberstock eight paintings for over 100,000 reichsmarks and all of them went to Linz. In addition, he arranged the consignment to Germany of other works of art bought by Haberstock elsewhere in Paris. It was Dequoy and his associate, Georges Destrem, who collaborated with Haberstock in arranging the sale of the Nicolas Rembrandts to Hitler and they did their utmost to acquire for the Fuehrer the massive Schloss collection at a time when it was being hidden from the Nazis in Vichy France.

There were many other important French dealers who sold to Haberstock paintings which later became part of the Linz collection. Herbert Engel of the Hugo Engel gallery acted as Haberstock's scout and agent in Nice where Haberstock made a profitable trip in the winter of 1940–41 with Posse's knowledge and approval. Through Engel, Haberstock made contact with Arthur Goldschmidt and bought from him 'Village Kermesse' by the seventeenth-century Flemish master Adriaen Brouwer, and 'Tavern Interior' by the Dutchman Adriaen van Ostade, recognized as Breughel's heir. Both paintings were subsequently bought by Hitler.

Extremely active in Paris on Haberstock's behalf was Madame Jane Weyll, friend of Baron von Poellnitz. She attended many of the auctions held at the Hotel Drouot and outbid a large number of dealers for the 'Annunciation' by the fifteenth-century Italian Renaissance painter, Andrea Solario. Haberstock had no trouble in selling this prize to Hitler. Madame Weyll played an active part in the 'Aryanization' of the Wildenstein gallery, thus preventing the Einsatzstab Rosenberg from confiscating any of its items which they could pass on to Goering. The Reich Marshal's wrath had to find an outlet and the unhappy victim was Madame Weyll's nobleman friend, who was a major in the Luftwaffe. In an attempt at placation, she offered Goering a portrait by Lucas Cranach which was owned by the Baron, fully aware of his great love for Cranach's works. But the quality of the picture was not good, the price was too high, and Goering turned it down. Later it was sold to Hitler for his Linz collection.

Haberstock cleverly exploited Hitler's generosity whenever

he was offered a painting he wanted. In June 1941 Haberstock bought seven paintings from the Wildenstein collection, paying a total of 46,500 reichsmarks. He got his money back from two of them, selling 'Battle on a Bridge' and 'Landscape with Nymphs', both by the French painter, Claude Lorrain, to Hitler for 48,000 reichsmarks. Two others, both portraits by Heinsius, Hitler bought for 10,000 and paid a further 5,500 for an eighteenth-century French mythological scene. Thus Haberstock found himself 17,000 reichsmarks in pocket and with still two paintings to sell—'Still life' by Jan Fyt and 'Two Nudes' by Gustave Courbet. The Fyt he never managed to sell but the Courbet figured in a most profitable exchange.

Haberstock had for many years maintained a close business relationship with a Lucerne dealer named Fischer whose representative in Germany was Carl Buemming of Darmstadt. After much negotiation, Haberstock obtained from Fischer two great Italian masterpieces—'Venus, Mars and Vulcan' by the Renaissance painter Paris Bordone, and Tintoretto's 'Lot and his Daughters'. As part of the payment, Haberstock gave the Courbet, which was later bought by the Berne Museum, and two early German panels. Hitler paid enormous sums for both the Italian works.

In his dealings with the Fuehrer, Haberstock worked on the principle that he was drawing money from a bottomless pit. He sold Hitler a Basaiti for 90,000 reichsmarks for which he had paid 67,500, a Ruisdael for 33,000 which cost him 18,000, and Breughel's 'Forest Road' for 32,500 against his own outlay of 20,000. In order to outbid all competitors at the Hotel Drouot for Solario's 'Annunciation', Madame Weyll was forced to go to 50,000 reichsmarks, but soon afterwards Haberstock sold it to Hitler for 72,500. On a Guardi he made more than 100 per cent profit, paying out 20,000 and persuading Hitler to buy it for 45,000.

After spending a lifetime in it, Haberstock was more aware than most that the art world was a jungle in which one had to be ruthless to survive. Unhesitatingly he threatened, cajoled, bullied and blackmailed, all on the basis of his personal relationship with the Fuehrer and his long membership of the party.

Often his intended victims were the German museums on whom he tried to foist inferior works by nineteenth-century German painters, such as Schuch and Truebner, in exchange for great masterpieces which he knew he could sell at a vast profit. His weapon was the threat of the State's disapproval of museums which retained paintings by artists not favoured by the Nazi leaders, and Haberstock was only too willing to help them out of this difficulty. He approached the Karlsruhe Museum and informed its Director, a man called Martin, that he was running considerable risk in housing paintings by the eighteenth-century French painter, Jean-Baptiste Chardin. He was willing to do him the favour of taking all the Chardins off his hands and filling the gaps on the walls with excellent Truebners, a painter much admired by the Fuehrer. Herr Martin had the sense and courage to refuse.

One of the greatest paintings held in any German museum was Holbein's 'Meyer Madonna' in the Schloss Museum at Darmstadt, painted about 1526. Since Holbein's death, Germany had failed to produce an artist of equal stature and Haberstock was determined to obtain this masterpiece by the Reich's last great painter, though he himself never expressed this view in Hitler's hearing. He wrote repeatedly to the Schloss Museum, refusing to take the inevitable 'No' as a final answer. In all his letters he claimed to be a 'serious prospective purchaser' and offered 'some property of corresponding value', meaning Spitzwegs and Truebners, which are like flickering candles against the brightness of Holbein's genius. But this time water did not wear away the stone, the museum turning a deaf ear to Haberstock's promises, cajolery, and dark hints.

As he grew older, Haberstock lived more and more in the past, drawing on his shared memories with the Fuehrer like capital withdrawn from a bank. But if others were forced to accept him on that account, they still did not trust him. They called him a 'pirate', 'a cunning shark'. As early as June 1940, Dr Hanssen, then Bormann's secretary, was expressing this general distrust in a report to his employer. Passes had been made available for Dr Posse to visit the Netherlands and other occupied countries, and Haberstock had offered to accompany him, suggesting that his personal knowledge of the art dealers in these countries would be invaluable. Posse had agreed but Dr Hanssen strongly opposed Haberstock going on the grounds that he would buy the best things, not Posse, and then sell them to the Fuehrer at inflated prices. Moreover, he claimed, every other German dealer would be enraged and demand passes also. Knowing Haberstock as well as they did, they were not prepared to grant him the slightest advantage.

Once Posse was no longer head of the Sonderauftrag Linz, Haberstock's power rapidly dwindled. Even Hitler became suspicious of the old fox. After his gallery at 59 Kurfuersten-strasse was destroyed during an air-raid on Berlin, Haberstock moved with his wife to a castle at Aschbach, owned by Baron von Poellnitz, the friend of his one-time Paris agent. There he spent the rest of the war in retirement, ageing rapidly, his teeth drawn.

CHAPTER SEVEN

Vandalism in the East

Being an ally of Nazi Germany did not place a nation's artistic treasures beyond the greedy reach of Hitler, Goering and other Nazi leaders. In Italy there was no organized looting as long as the Axis survived but it commenced after September 1943, the month in which Italian resistance collapsed, leaving the Germans in control of Northern Italy and placing the magnificent art galleries of Florence at their mercy. While Mussolini was his Axis partner Hitler obtained masterpieces from Italy by buying them. His purchases were on such a scale that on 9 May 1942 Bottai, Minister of National Education in Mussolini's Government, was forced to publish a new law restricting the exportation of works of art.

Hans Posse concentrated a great deal of his energies on Italy, seeing it on a par with France as the major source of Europe's art treasures. He made three trips to Italy in 1941 alone, each thoroughly prepared by the energetic scouting of his main agent, Prince Philipp von Hessen.

Von Hessen, born in 1896, was a descendant of Queen Victoria and Emperor Frederick III of Prussia. He inherited the title of Oberpraesident of Hesse-Nassau and was educated at Frankfurt, Oxford, and Potsdam. Deciding to be an architect, he settled in Italy as a young man of twenty-six and joined the Fascist Party after the March on Rome. Later he offered his services to the Nazis, becoming an active exponent of National Socialism in Italy, and eventually being rewarded with the appointment of S.A. Lieutenant-General. Three years after settling in Italy he married Princess Malfada, second daughter of King Victor Emmanuel.

Von Hessen flourished until the end of 1943 when he fell foul of Hitler, though he was unable to discover the reasons for his loss of favour. At that time Hitler was sleeping badly and would order people to talk to him at all hours of the night. Von Hessen arrived at Hitler's headquarters one night after such a summons and stayed with the Fuehrer until two in the morning but was given no indication that anything was wrong. As he left to walk back to his own quarters, however, two Gestapo men approached him and placed him under arrest. He spent the next year in the Flossenburg concentration camp where his cousin, also a prisoner, would not talk to him because of von Hessen's past Nazi sympathies.

While in the camp early in 1945 he collapsed on being informed of his wife's death in an Allied air raid some six weeks earlier. He was later transferred to the Italian Tyrol, where he was kept under house arrest until his capture by the Americans.

Von Hessen was invaluable to Posse because of his wide knowledge of Italian painting and his acquaintanceship with numerous Italian art dealers. Posse made his first visit to Rome in March 1941, a few days after an order issued by Dr Lammers in Berlin opening an account of 500,000 reichsmarks in his name at the German Embassy in Rome. This first purchasing trip lasted two weeks and, even for Posse, it was extremely active. He returned to Dresden with a glowing opinion of his guide and adviser, and delighted with his acquisitions. On 23 March he wrote to Bormann:

I hereby report that the day before yesterday I returned from a 14-day trip to Italy.

Thanks to the preliminary work of Prince Philipp von Hessen, with whom I travelled to Rome (twice), Naples, Florence (twice), Turin and Genoa, I was able to acquire some 25 paintings for the Fuehrer. Among these are an important unknown painting by Tintoretto (dated 1562), paintings by Moroni, Salviati, Filippo Mazzola, Macrino d'Alba (large altarpiece), Pontormo, several works by Strozzi, Maratta, Castiglione, Amigoni, an early life-size portrait by Waldmueller of the wife of the composer, Rossini, full-length in an interior (approx 1831) and so on.

Several other things, some of them important, are still under discussion. I must say I am extremely happy to have the co-operation of Prince von Hessen, and that in addition to his good taste and his knowledge of art, his influential connexions with reference to purchases in Italy are very welcome indeed.

I have run out of money kept for my disposal in Rome for new Italian purchases. I have already approached Dr Lammers to replenish the account at the German Embassy in Rome. . . .

To get through half a million reichsmarks on a fortnight's trip was big spending even for Dr Posse. Only six days after writing his letter to Bormann, he received an urgent telegram from the Prince, asking him to return to Rome without delay. Von Hessen had discovered a number of further masterpieces which he felt sure would interest the Fuehrer. Posse hurriedly arranged another visa and two days later was sending an urgent request from Rome for more money. It took Dr Lammers only a matter of hours, urged on by Bormann acting on Hitler's instructions, to open a second account for Posse of half a million reichsmarks in Rome. Again it was quickly spent and the latest batch of paintings sent back into Germany.

Posse made a third trip to Italy on 3 June. Von Hessen had promised that it would be so successful that eight days before leaving Dresden, Posse wrote to Bormann, outlining the preparations ambitious enough to measure up to his optimism:

By previous arrangement with Oberpraesident Prince Philipp von Hessen, I leave for Italy on 3 June for about a week. At midnight on 3/4 June a special train for the transport of pictures will be ready in Munich to leave for Italy. It will travel via Milan, then Bologna-Florence-Rome.

As in the next few days I shall have to make all preparations, I should thank you for letting me know whether I must buy a ticket when going by special train or if this is not necessary.

Secondly, since the Dresden-Munich railroad connexions are extremely difficult, I should be particularly obliged if there was an opportunity to take me by plane on 3 June from the Dresden airfield (Klotzsche) to Munich so that I can make connexion with the special train in Munich on 4 June at 12.40 a.m.

With such riches promised, Bormann was only too willing to accede to this request. Posse caught his special plane and travelled on his special train to Rome. While there, he wrote again to Bormann, warning him that further funds would be needed in the near future. These were not forthcoming at once but Bormann revealed how generous the Fuehrer could be in a letter sent to Dr Posse on 28 June, soon after his return to Dresden:

I have given orders for increasing the special account at the German Embassy in Rome for the use of Prince Philipp von Hessen by the amount of 13,200,000 lire (1,650,000 reichsmarks) and have requested the Foreign Office to instruct the German Embassy to make payments, if necessary in advance of the transfer of foreign exchange, from the Reichminister of Economy to their own treasury. Afterwards, when the account is closed, I request that you present an accounting with bills and photographs of the acquired works of art, and at the same time indicate the use to be made of each item.

Unlike Paris, there was to be no competition with Goering in Rome by Hitler's request. Both Posse and von Hessen were given strict instructions not to approach the Italian art dealer, Contini Bonacossi, who had sold more than fifty paintings to the Reich Marshal. Even with these limitations, the haul was prodigious in quality. Acting on his own while other Linz affairs tied Posse down to his desk in Dresden, Prince Philipp bought for Hitler eighty-eight major works of art, mostly paintings, which were delivered to the Fuehrerbau and catalogued by Reger. Probably the most important was 'Portrait of a Man in a Black Cap' by Hans Memling, who was born in Germany in the fifteenth century but spent his life as an artist in Bruges. With Hitler's full authority, von Hessen opened negotiations with Prince Corsini in Florence, owner of the Memling. The price finally agreed was over five million lire and the picture was handed over. More than twenty years later it is one of the many great masterpieces still to be traced, either having been mysteriously destroyed or hidden away in some private collection.

Other paintings purchased by the Prince would grace any of the world's museums. They included a portrait of two men by Tintoretto, another portrait by Titian, a large Pannini landscape, 'Leda' by Leonardo da Vinci, a Canaletto landscape, two Raphaels, an equestrian portrait by Rubens which was also purchased in Florence, 'Portrait of Giovanni Grassi' by Pietro Longhi, a portrait by the Italian Renaissance painter Lorenzo Lotto, two paintings by the great Venetian, Giandomenico Tiepolo, a portrait of a bearded man by Francesco Mazzola, also known as Parmigianino, and Tintoretto's 'Entombment of Christ', one of his tremendous dramatic paintings.

Besides collaborating with his favourite Prince in buying numerous masterpieces for the Fuehrer, Dr Posse was also drawn into the long-standing quarrel over the Italian South Tyrol which the Nazis regarded as belonging to the Reich. Under the German-Italian agreement of 21 October 1939 the Italians had agreed that valuable objects of German culture and art should be returned to Germany. These included tomb monuments, private collections and archives relating to German culture, and museum articles of German origin. Early in 1940 Himmler had reported on the problem to Bormann, stating that though the Italians had made far-reaching concessions on paper, little progress had been made in returning to Germany those valuable works of art that rightfully belonged to the Reich.

Himmler had set up a commission called the 'Ahnenerbe' (hereditary property) to look after German interests. As further proof that Hitler had decided from the beginning that he would dominate any art looting carried out by the leading Nazis, Himmler reported to Bormann:

> My deputy in the South Tyrol has been instructed to see to it that art objects which are privately owned are not sold to unauthorized persons, and that first option is reserved for the Fuehrer on all oil paintings coming into Germany.

Posse appeared on the scene when he was appointed art adviser to the Ahnenerbe and while on one of his 1941 buying trips with Prince Philipp, he spent two days at Bolzano in the South Tyrol, discussing with Ahnenerbe officials the question of returning art treasures of German origin. He told Bormann by letter: 'The difficulties, which are made in this connexion from the Italian side, are tremendous. . . .' Posse made little progress in solving the problem but later when Italy's collapse was the signal for systematic looting by the Germans, the Ahnenerbe came into its own. It served as a cover for the seizure of Italian works of art, and the South Tyrol became the largest storehouse of German loot. One of the biggest repositories for works of art was the castle of San Leonardo di Passiria at San Leonardo, while Campo Tures was used to store paintings looted from the Uffizi, the Pitti Palace and other Florentine galleries.

Though he had a high opinion of Prince Philipp von Hessen, Posse did not deal entirely through him. He made several purchases on his own for Linz while in Italy, including a Rubens portrait and 'Christ Carrying the Cross' by Tiepolo. He also sought no help in his attempt to seize Makart's great triptych, 'The Plague in Florence', housed in Florence in the villa of the Landau-Finaly family, who are related to the Rothschilds. As early as September 1940 Posse wrote to Bormann, drawing his attention to the sequestration of the Landau-Finaly villa by the Italian authorities. He added:

> In the same villa is Makart's 'The Plague of Florence' for

which we have repeatedly negotiated. Perhaps we can now acquire this painting through diplomatic channels.

But for once Bormann was ahead of the Fuehrer's chief art adviser. Six days later he replied to Posse in the shortest of notes:

The sequestration of the Florentine villa was done by our recommendation; the necessary steps for acquiring the painting have already been taken.

Officially the Makart was entered in the Linz records as 'a present from the Duce'. It was considered by Hitler as one of his greatest captures, a happy omen that his dreams for Linz would be fulfilled. He was so delighted that he exhibited the Makart twice at the Fuehrerbau, once when it was delivered and again in the following November when select invitations went out for a special viewing. When Heinrich Hoffmann's article on the Linz collection appeared in the *Kunst dem Volk* in 1943, the Makart was reproduced in colour as one of the major illustrations. Before the war Karl Haberstock had tried to buy it but had been told by the Landau-Finaly family that it was not for sale and never would be sold.

The Makart was not the only painting given by Mussolini to Hitler. One other gift between the two dictators was a large painting of classical ruins by Giovanni Pannini. Goering also presented Hitler with some of his Italian purchases, including two views of the interior of St Peter's, also by Pannini, for which Goering had paid 250,000 lire (31,000 reichsmarks).

As long as Italy was an ally, even though also too often a liability, Hitler was prepared to contain his own avidity and that of the other Nazi leaders for her magnificent art collections. He made no protest when the May 1942 decree virtually reduced German buying to a trickle. But the Allied invasion of the toe of Italy and the fall of Mussolini transformed the situation. As the armies under General Alexander began their painful advance, the directors of the Italian art galleries began to evacuate their treasures, storing them in remote villas, farmhouses, castles and monasteries, not at first fully appreciating that their real enemy was behind them.

The Nazis' first big target were the two major collections from Naples moved to the expected calm and peacefulness of the monastery of Monte Cassino. Before the massive Allied bombardment began, the Germans announced that they were moving the collections on to the Vatican for greater safety. Some paintings did arrive but many others were looted en route by various S.S. officers, two of them—a Titian and a Claude Lorrain—being presented to Goering as birthday presents. Another seventeen paintings and various bronzes unexpectedly turned up at Karinhall but for once Goering's acute embarrassment overcame his collector's passion and he hurriedly forwarded them to Berlin. Details of them were shown to Hitler and he ordered them to be stored at Alt Aussee with a view to adding them to the Linz collection.

Looting went on throughout Northern Italy. Famous art galleries were ransacked by German soldiers before they retreated farther northwards. The greatest single haul was achieved by the German 362nd Infantry Division in July 1944 which removed 307 paintings from Florentine galleries, including the Uffizi and the Pitti. They were stored away in various caches in South Tyrol in the summer months of 1944, but when the Germans were forced to abandon even this area, they departed so hurriedly that most of the art treasures were left behind. At Campo Tures there were so many crates of priceless canvases that they were even piled high in a garage. Another Nazi storehouse for their Italian loot was the salt-mine at Bad Aussee, near Salzburg.

If the Italians, by their mass surrenders, had shown they had little heart for becoming cannon-fodder in what most of them regarded as a futile war, there was no lack of courage in their attempts to regain their national art treasures. They saw more sense in fighting for a Titian or a Tintoretto than for a desolate piece of waste-ground that was no use to anyone. Acting on the suggestion of the great philosopher, Benedetto Croce, the new Italian Government in Naples headed by Marshal Badoglio found no difficulty in obtaining volunteers amongst the Army's ranks to infiltrate behind the German lines in order to discover what art treasures were being looted and where they were being taken. Some of them were caught and died but others brought back valuable information which made much easier the task of the Fine Arts Sub-Commission, set up by the Allied Military Government to recover missing works of art as the last German soldier finally quit Italian soil.

Much was recovered, but many great paintings are still missing. Post-war estimates put the number of paintings looted by the German armies in Italy at about 3,600, many of them worth a fortune. Some 600 are still missing. These include three important collections—the Perugia collection of the eminent historian Van Marle; the Mason Perkins collection which contains a number of Italian primitives; and the collection of the Bourbon-Parma family. Notable art works still to be traced are a head of a faun sculptured by Michelangelo when he was only fifteen, a Madonna and Child by Pierino da Vainci, the Memling portrait, and a still life by Jan van Huysum.

As an ex-enemy, Italy had a hard fight to obtain rights equal to the other occupied countries. The peace treaty barred her from any war reparation claims against Germany but in 1948 it was amended to give Italy equal rights in the restitution of art treasures. Many of her national works of art were found at Alt Aussee, in Berchtesgaden and on Goering's Karinhall estate. But the 1948 amendment did not mark the end of the struggle, many Germans claiming that the great art treasures bought in Italy by Hitler, Goering and other Nazi leaders had been legally purchased and therefore should remain in Germany. Protests from German artists and scholars went as far as President Truman but in 1953 the Adenauer Government wisely decided otherwise, and the process began of handing back to the Italians more than 300 paintings bought by the Nazi leaders and often illegally exported. Six years later the process was complete.

The search for the 600 canvases amongst the other lost art treasures still goes on. Many are believed to have changed hands several times. Two of them by Pollaiuolo, the fifteenth-century Italian painter, turned up in California but most of them are thought to be still in Germany, hidden in bank vaults or

private homes. They cannot be sold without their owners
running the greatest risks.

*

While Italy was still a viable member of the Axis and looting
by the Nazis was strictly forbidden, eastwards Hitler was
carrying out a policy of wanton destruction and desecration.
Every occupied country in Western Europe had contributed
some of its art treasures towards the Linz collection but none
came from Russia because Hitler believed nothing of any cultural value could exist in a country which he had always thought
it was his destiny to destroy. He looked upon Bolshevism with a
blazing hatred and saw the Russians as a sub-human species to
be destroyed as vermin. Not even his passion to make the Linz
collection the greatest in the world could modify or reduce his
hatred and many great art treasures in Russia worthy of any collection were senselessly destroyed as hatred obliterated greed.
Nothing that happened in Western Europe can be compared
with the Nazi barbarism towards great works of art exhibited in
Russia.

Even before the German troops had crossed on to Russian
soil in June 1941, Hitler decided that the organization of looting
should be the responsibility of Einsatzstab Rosenberg. Two
months before the invasion Rosenberg was ready to move his
staff eastwards under the command of Gerhardt Utikal, his
chief of staff. But like every other Nazi commander in Russia,
Rosenberg badly underestimated the immensity of the task facing
him and as the German divisions swept forward, occupying a
vast area of land yielded by the ill-organized Russian troops, it
became painfully clear that the Einsatzstab was far too small to
cope with the problem, even though the main policy was brutal
pillaging and burning by German troops acting barbarously
because they believed they were dealing with a barbaric people.

In the August, three months after the invasion, Hitler decided it was time to intervene. He relieved Rosenberg of the
burden of his Russian operations, for which the latter was not
ungrateful, and ordered von Ribbentrop to carry out the

systematic looting of Russian towns and cities. Even if none of the loot was worthy of being set aside for Linz, there was no reason why other Nazis shouldn't enjoy the fruits of conquest.

Hitler's precise orders to von Ribbentrop were that he was 'to seize and secure immediately after the fall of large cities and towns their cultural centres and all objects of great historical value, to select valuable books and films, and finally dispatch all seizures to Germany'. But as the fighting reached a savage intensity, as great armies became locked together and the piles of German dead mounted higher and higher, these orders were forgotten and the Ribbentrop battalions were swept aside. German officers made no attempt to restrain their troops from desecrating what was sacred in Russian eyes and embarking on an orgy of destruction.

In an attempt to carry out the Fuehrer's orders, von Ribbentrop organized four battalions under his personal direction. He set up headquarters at 104 Hermann Goering Strasse in Berlin and appointed Major von Konsberg of the Waffen S.S. as commanding officer.

One of the four battalions was assigned to work with Rommel in North Africa. The other three were sent to Russia, one each attached to the Army Group North, Army Group Centre, and Army Group South. They were told that all looted works of art were to be sent to the Adler premises in the Hardenbergstrasse in Berlin where they would be classified and catalogued. As the trainloads of loot reached Berlin, Hitler maintained his indifference, refusing to be shown the photograph of any outstanding work of art that might be worthy of Linz or to order Posse to carry out a tour of inspection.

The three von Ribbentrop battalions carried out their allotted tasks with methodical efficiency. The Second Battalion looted and pillaged the palaces in the Leningrad suburbs while the battle to capture the heart of the city still raged. Great rooms were stripped bare as paintings, sculptures, tapestries, and ornaments were roughly piled together, ready for transport to Germany. Little notice was taken if a beautiful vase was dropped and smashed to pieces or a fine painting ripped beyond repair, while only loud laughter greeted a German boot wantonly kicked through a canvas. The palace and museum of the Empress Catherine were ransacked. Chinese silk draperies and carved gilt ornaments were torn down from the walls, and anything of value was carted away. In the palace of the Emperor Alexander the large collection of antique furniture was shipped to Germany as well as the large library, containing 7,000 volumes in French and 5,000 in Russian. Like a plague of locusts, the Germans descended upon Leningrad and stripped bare the land.

The Fourth Battalion extended the scope of its operations beyond palaces. It entered the laboratories of the Medical and Scientific Research Institute at Kiev and methodically packed every piece of equipment, book and document for dispatch to Germany. Likewise it picked clean the Ukrainian Academy of Science, the Kiev Museum of Ukrainian, Russian and Western Art, the central Schevtchenko museum and the Korolenko library in Kharkov. Not only was every painting taken from the Kharkov art gallery but von Ribbentrop's men even stole the fittings, such as curtains and carpets. In Kiev more than four million books, magazines and manuscripts, most of them rare and some even unique, were looted by the Germans. Rare works of art were looted from the palaces of Peterhof, Tsarskoye Selo and Pavlosk.

Five months after the invasion Reich Commissar Kube could report that the value of works of art looted from Byelorussia ran into millions of roubles. Freight cars packed with loot from Russia reached Germany at the rate of forty to fifty a month, most of it being roughly sorted in East Prussia before it was moved on to Berlin and other German cities.

With looting there is the hope of possible restitution once a war is over. Far worse is the deliberate and wanton destruction of things of great beauty which are lost to the world for ever. Throughout Russia the Germans methodically destroyed a total of 427 museums, including those at Leningrad, Smolensk, Stalingrad, Novgorod and Poltava. In Western Europe by comparison, some museums were destroyed during bombing attacks but very few were deliberately razed to the ground by occupying German troops.

As bad as the destruction was the desecration carried out in Russia. At Mikhailovskoye the estate of the poet Pushkin was broken up, his grave desecrated, and neighbouring villages and the near-by Svyatogor monastery burned to the ground. Tolstoy's Yasnaya Polyana estate was also destroyed and his grave desecrated. In addition the Germans reduced to rubble the Tchaikovsky museum at Klin and the museum of the painter Repin at Penaty.

The story of German vandalism in Russia is a terrible one, not all of which has been made known to the West. What the Russians have revealed of the terrible wounds they suffered from German hands is ample proof of the depths to which the Nazis could sink when the viciousness that was always just below the surface was allowed to reign unchecked. Hitler was uninterested in Russian art treasures and made no attempt to check their wilful destruction. He was uncaring and, without control from the top, barbarism became inevitable in a war where the deaths ran into millions, prisoners on both sides were shot out of hand and the Russians scorched their own land so that German troops should freeze to death as they were caught by the bitter cold of a Russian winter.

Paradoxically, the events in Russia give reason for the West to be grateful that Adolf Hitler was obsessed with his Linz dream. Because he was determined to build, as have all dictators in history, a great monument to his own glory, he looted and illegally purchased on a large scale, but what passed into his hands was carefully stored away. Throughout the chain of command he made explicit his wish to have first claim on any great work of art seized in the occupied countries. He exercised personal control so that no Nazi barbarian in Western Europe—and there were many—would dare wantonly to destroy a masterpiece by Rembrandt, Rubens or Tintoretto without risking his neck. In addition, minor Nazi officials soon learned that works of art were a valuable currency because they were the means of currying favour with the Fuehrer and other Nazi leaders. Even when the mounting aerial bombardment of Germany presented a new danger, Hitler took energetic steps to ensure that the masterpieces collected by himself, Goering, and

Alfred Rosenberg, director of the main Nazi looting organization in Paris who sided with Goering in his rivalry with Hitler to obtain the great masterpieces. He was hanged at Nuremberg as a war criminal

(*Above*): 'The Last Supper', painted by the fifteenth-century Netherlands painter, Dirk Bouts, for the Church of St Peter at Louvain; hidden at Alt Aussee

Michelangelo's masterpiece, the Madonna and Child, was looted by the Germans from the Church of Notre-Dame in Bruges and transported across Europe

Botticelli's 'Simonetta', purchased by Hitler in 1938 for 300,000
reichsmarks from the dealer Walter Bornheim after a plot claiming that
it was irreparably damaged

A bust of Karl Haberstock, the German art dealer who made a fortune out of selling Hitler pictures for his Linz collections

Dr Hermann Voss, Director of the Wiesbaden Gallery, who succeeded Dr Posse as head of the Sonderauftrag Linz, though with considerably reduced powers

The van Eyck brothers' 'Adoration of the Lamb', painted in 1432 for the Cathedral of St Bavon at Ghent: hidden at Alt Aussee

Schloss Weesenstein, near Dresden, where Hitler stored large numbers of prints and drawings. The building was taken by the Russians in 1945

The Meyer Madonna by Holbein, part of the Schloss Museum collection at Darmstadt, one of the few masterpieces admired by Hitler which he was never able to obtain

Hermann Goering and Prince Philipp von Hessen, who became the main Linz agent in Italy, buying numerous paintings for Hitler. He was a descendant of Emperor Frederick III of Prussia and Queen Victoria

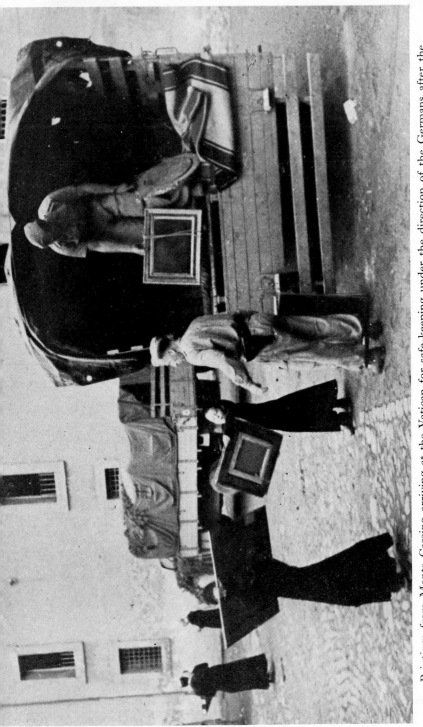

Paintings from Monte Cassino arriving at the Vatican for safe-keeping under the direction of the Germans after the collapse of Italy. Many others were looted en route

The creation of Mad Ludwig of Bavaria, Schloss Neuschwanstein became a vast treasure-house when it was chosen as the main repository of the Einsatzstab Rosenberg

A miscellaneous collection of art treasures in a typical storeroom in the Schloss Neuschwanstein

Bad Aussee in the Austrian Alps, some seventy miles south-east of
Salzburg and only a few miles from the Alt Aussee salt-mine

The administration buildings of the Alt Aussee salt-mine taken over by
the Nazis as the final main repository for Hitler's vast Linz collection

Panels of the Ghent altarpiece stored underground at Alt Aussee. On the left is the art restorer Karl Sieber, who did more than anyone to prevent the mine being blown up

One of the large chambers in the Alt Aussee salt-mine, divided by stout storage racks. In the foreground a hygrometer to check the humidity of the air

The Madonna and Child being carefully hauled out of the Alt Aussee salt-mine by uniformed American art experts. It was restored to Bruges in September 1945

The slow proc of reparation. Recovered art treasures were stored in racks the Central Collecting Poir in Munich befe their rightful owners were discovered

Heinrich Hoffm Hitler's official photographer, after his captur by the Allies ir 1945

others were buried deep, out of the bombers' reach. The notorious raid on Dresden may have killed 100,000 people, but before it happened, the city's many art treasures had been moved to a place of safety, which was in Hitler's eyes more important than the men, women, and children of Dresden.

There can be very little doubt that if Hitler and Goering had been indifferent to the art treasures of Western Europe, the events in Russia would have been repeated, even though perhaps on a lesser scale. Minor Nazi thugs would have senselessly destroyed a great masterpiece simply because other men thought it beautiful. They would have needed no other reason. The cultural heritage of Western Europe was spared such horrors because of the Linz dream.

*

Having ordered the burning of books during the days of his rise to power, Hitler decided that he wanted to collect them. If Linz was to have the greatest art gallery in Western Europe, it must also have the greatest library. He planned it as part of the Sonderauftrag Linz, but distinct from the museum collections which came under Posse's jurisdiction. Though it would accommodate all branches of literature, Hitler saw his Linz library as being the seat of knowledge of the National Socialist movement, containing the truths of the world as he saw them.

He delayed making any move to organize the library until he had found the right man to create it exactly as he wanted it. In April 1941 he decided he had found that man and instructed Bormann to write to Dr Friedrich Wolffhardt, suggesting that he might make some purchases for the 'Neue Linzer Bibliothek' even though, as yet, no plans for the building had been drawn up. Wolffhardt was then forty-two, an active party member, close friend of Bormann and Dr Helmut von Hummel, who was later to succeed Dr Hanssen as Bormann's right-hand man. Wolffhardt possessed all the qualifications necessary for a librarian. He had a regard for books, possessed an extremely orderly mind, and was a highly efficient administrator. He kept a detailed diary, never allowed his files to become more than a few days out of date, and answered promptly all his correspondence.

Though the request was only that he should buy some books, Wolffhardt was shrewd enough to guess that he was being tested for bigger things. Through his friendship with Bormann he was well aware that the Linz library project was in the offing and he knew, without being vain, that it would suit his talents admirably. Deciding that his best plan was to force the issue, Wolffhardt worked throughout that summer on an elaborate system of proposals for the Linz library, outlining its various sections. He dismissed peremptorily the idea of knowledge for knowledge's sake. He wanted the library to be totally pro-Nazi by eliminating all subversive literature, even if written by the greatest authors and demonstrating that it could be a complete expression of National Socialist ideology. He had no doubt that his proposals would appeal to the Fuehrer.

Wolffhardt made only one mistake. Being neat and pedantic, his handwriting was likewise, the letters small and the lines close together. He also found satisfaction in filling every inch of space, disliking waste of any kind, even of only parts of a sheet of notepaper. He submitted his report and on 21 August received a reply from Bormann at his home at 10 Ruffinstrasse in Munich. Bormann wrote revealingly:

> I have received the draft of your memorandum. . . . I should like to submit it to the Fuehrer but in the present form this is impossible because, neatly as you have written it on transparent paper, the draft is not legible enough for the Fuehrer. First of all, the Fuehrer, who has been working and reading for many hours until late at night, has already ruined his eyes and, secondly, we can only work by electric light in the air-raid shelter of our Fuehrer HQ which makes reading still more difficult. The draft must be copied on thicker paper by a typewriter with large type, on one side of the paper only and triple-spaced. . . .

Wolffhardt hastened to carry out these instructions. The new version of the report was eighty pages long and legible enough to be read by Hitler, who gave it his immediate approval. Wolffhardt was appointed Director of the Linz library on a par with Dr Posse in the Sonderauftrag and answerable directly to Bormann. By September he had moved into the office made available for him in the Fuehrerbau and started the tasks which were to occupy all his energies for the next three and a half years.

Posse accepted the position, being fully occupied with his own tasks. He took part in the affairs of the library briefly when there was a discussion as to the distribution of the Rothschild books, confiscated many months previously. Bormann decided that they should go to the Vienna National Library but any duplicates should be given to Linz. On 3 October 1941, while travelling on Hitler's special train, he wrote to Wolffhardt that the Fuehrer only wanted to purchase 'really valuable literature', particularly such books which 'we shall not be able to get easily later on'. He expressed the confident view that in due time valuable books from all the great libraries of Europe would be added to the Linz collection.

By 1942 Wolffhardt was energetically buying books from all parts of Europe. Though Bormann held the purse-strings, he was extremely generous. When Wolffhardt sent in a request for 30,000 reichsmarks for a particular purchase, Bormann wrote back that he could have ten times that amount. Wolffhardt was given a completely free hand as to the purchases he made within Germany itself.

Wolffhardt proved himself as tireless as Dr Posse. He found time to discuss the plans for the Linz library with a Munich architect. He obeyed a request from Bormann to co-operate with Dr Leopold Ruprecht, in charge of the Linz armour collection, by supplying him with the literature that would help him to make the best possible acquisitions. He toured Europe, examining books and valuable manuscripts, making several trips to neutral Switzerland.

Extracts from his diary illuminate his activities. After a visit from Carl Buemming, the Darmstadt art dealer, Wolffhardt wrote:

For the Stifter collection the owner asks 5,500 Swiss francs. There are various possibilities of purchasing this collection without foreign currency, but they are all complicated and dubious as to result. The best solution would be to find a German of the Reich in Switzerland, willing to donate in advance the money.

According to Buemming's estimate, the collection today represents a market-value of 6,700 reichsmarks. It would be fairly acceptable to purchase it for 5,500 Swiss francs. Buemming, on the one hand, will try to reduce the owner's demand and, on the other hand, will keep in view completion of the purchase on the aforementioned basis.

We talked about the Toepfer library....

This latter had been previously bought by Hitler for 65,000 Swiss francs. It had been owned by a Dr Toepfer of Lucerne and Buemming's commission, as agent, had been 6,500 reichsmarks.

Wolffhardt continued:

Eventually Buemming informed me confidentially of the Gutmann library in Vienna. It had been safeguarded by the Fuehrer together with other valuable art property of Gutmann in Vienna. The Jew Gutmann is in America. His daughter [Baroness Ferstel] has contrived to obtain the precious Duerer collection through various intrigues but there still exists a Rembrandt collection.

Mr B. suggests that the library with its valuable French 17th and 18th century books be sold at auction, e.g. in Lucerne through Hoepli-Milan, in order thus to provide the Reich with foreign currency. The total value of the library is likely to amount to 500,000 Swiss francs....

But these plans did not materialize. The Gutmann collection was kept by Hitler in Vienna until Allied air attacks forced him to remove it to the Alt Aussee mine.

Wolffhardt also became interested in the Neufforge collection, held by the widowed Baroness Neufforge in Berne. He instructed Buemming to contact her to see if she would be willing to sell. He wrote in his diary:

> Today Buemming and Mrs Zalenka called on me. We discussed the Neufforge collection. Both the Neufforges, husband and wife, are said to be smart and greedy people, not idealists. Baron N. is said to have expressed the wish that the library should be turned over to the Art-Ancienne, though that institution is till today half-Jewish. Mrs Zalenka stated that during the Truebner auction in 1939, Baron N. had made deprecatory remarks about politics.

But whatever the dead Baron had said in 1939, his library was still frustratingly beyond Wolffhardt's reach. After Buemming had failed to make any progress, he decided to go to Berne himself. Wolffhardt stayed about twelve days, half-way through his visit suffering the indignity of having to go to Lucerne to apply for an extension of his residence permit. He was by no means welcomed by the Swiss authorities. His first three days in Berne he spent visiting a public exhibition of the Neufforge collection. He noted in his diary:

> The books exhibited are extremely beautiful examples. On one wall Neufforge's specially designed display shelves, in the middle of the display tables of the library, on two walls single sheet publications under glass.

His visits increased his determination to buy the collection but he found even seeing the Baroness most difficult. On the tenth day he was at last granted an interview at her pension in Berne and found her accompanied by Count Scherin. Wolffhardt was at his most persuasive but he made little impression on the Baroness. That night he wrote in his diary:

> The Baroness appeared rather disinclined to sell. The library is to remain with the family, more so as the stepson is ready to take it over. We suggested that on the one hand such a voluminous treasure of books should belong—from the

cultural standpoint—to the general public, and, on the other hand, it could be hardly maintained as private property in view of the cost of maintenance.

We intimated that the payment could be arranged largely according to the family's convenience, also in form of rent. Buemming will discuss the matter with the family lawyer. On this occasion details of what they ask may be learned.

His forebodings proved correct. He made several more approaches but all his offers, eloquence, and desire to be accommodating had no effect on the Baroness, who wasn't selling anything to Adolf Hitler. On the twelfth day he entered three glum words in his diary: 'Return to Munich.' His colossal bid of a million reichsmarks for the Neufforge collection had failed.

But elsewhere he could produce an impressive string of successes. In an inventory compiled by Wolffhardt and going up to 30 November 1943, he claimed to have spent 343,194 reichsmarks on books, magazines, and manuscripts. Two-thirds of this sum had been spent in the previous six months, mostly inside Germany. Wolffhardt was also negotiating for the Klinckowstroem collection, valued at 70,000 reichsmarks, a collection of old books in Leipzig, valued at 100,000 reichsmarks, and was bidding at least 50,000 for a collection about to be auctioned in Holland. In addition, he had received another 746 rare volumes as presents, obtained by Bormann through the Party Chancelleries in Berlin and Munich.

Wolffhardt reported that he had spent a great deal on scientific books, less on first editions and fine illustrated works. He had paid out a further 69,256 reichsmarks for music manuscripts and books, some of considerable importance, but added that foreign currency obstacles had caused several Swiss sales to be called off, even where objects of unquestionable importance to the Reich were concerned. Wolffhardt concluded his inventory:

Considering that we have 20,000 items, apart from those on the way and still more expected, the employment of ten trained librarians and five to ten book-binders would not be too much for taking care of this literature. Additional materials and facilities would be indispensable.

The war in its present hard form makes me waive any request for an enlargement of the project. We are doing here what we can, and this is no more than our duty.

Wolffhardt was reporting from the Villa Castiglione at Grundlsee, Upper Danube, where he had moved with his family and staff in April 1943 to escape Allied air attacks. Obtained through party channels, the villa was a large, well-appointed mansion that served as a central collecting point for the Linz library. Every book received was card catalogued and inventoried by a clerical staff under Dr Ludwig Lang. Afterwards they were sent to various repositories, the most important being Hohenfurth. The correspondence, accounts, and other records of the library remained at the villa, where Wolffhardt could have them tidily at his finger-tips.

Three months after his inventory he was able to report that his collection had reached 40,000 volumes with another 250,000 under negotiation. In 1944 his expenditure jumped to 584,776 reichsmarks and he still went on buying in 1945, almost until the day Germany decided he could better serve his country in uniform.

Wolffhardt, who was made an S.S. Captain early in 1942, had no scruples about confiscating books and seldom gave up once he had tracked down a collection he wanted. His greatest frustrations were in Switzerland, his greatest successes in Austria, where he found Vienna a particularly rich source. He plundered large and small libraries, living completely inside a world whose walls were made of books.

Late in the war he discovered evidence of looting by security policemen in provincial Austria. In Styria the library of a not unimportant Aryan scholar had been burned. In Lower Styria the security services had seized an instruction book for the violin by Leopold Mozart and a volume by Copernicus from private collections and both, Wolffhardt feared, had been converted into cash. Libraries at places like Admont and St

Lamprecht had been looted of considerable stocks without the local Gauleiter doing anything to prevent it.

Wolffhardt catalogued his woes in a report to Bormann, who was far more concerned with the twilight of Nazi Germany than what might be happening in a few unimportant libraries. Receiving no reply, Wolffhardt grumpily asked how he could be expected to build the greatest library in Europe with such lack of co-operation.

CHAPTER EIGHT

The Death of Hans Posse

After years of driving himself too hard, the health of Dr Hans Posse began to fail towards the end of 1942. His illness rapidly developed but although he was in great pain, he worked on with a fanatical energy, carrying out further buying trips, completing further purchases, seeing dozens of people every day. He had entered Hitler's imagination and become obsessed with the same vision that existed only as jigsaw pieces hidden in a dozen different storehouses and recorded only in the complicated filing system of Hans Reger.

In his diary on 20 November 1942 Dr Wolffhardt noted:

> Director Posse is in bad shape, but he is working and receiving visitors. His co-worker, Dr Reimer, is informed of everything.

Dr Gottfried Reimer was a man in his early thirties. Dark and of medium height, he had been employed in museums in Vienna before coming to Dresden to work with Posse in his gallery. He was quiet, aloof, and showed no liking for the Nazi Party. Early in June 1941 Posse appointed him as his administrative assistant, keeping Reimer informed of what was going on so that he could keep the wheels turning while Posse was away on buying trips. As Posse's fatal illness progressed

Reimer's role grew in stature, but Posse did not propose his name or any other to Hitler as his possible successor. By refusing to discuss the question, he was denying its existence. He kept on working each day round the clock until the energy and willpower finally drained from his body. By the middle of December he was dead from cancer of the mouth.

Hitler ordered an impressive funeral. By order of the Fuehrer, every museum director in Germany was compelled to attend, walking in slow procession behind the bier, each man wondering if he would get the job. As proof of the party's high regard for the dead man, the eulogy was read by Dr Goebbels, who praised him extravagantly, saying how he laid down his life for his country as any soldier at the front. Other Nazi leaders added their tributes, but the man who owed Hans Posse more than anyone else was not present. The running of the war at the watershed between victory and defeat was occupying all Adolf Hitler's time.

Up to now the Sonderauftrag Linz had been largely the work of one man. Though Hitler had supplied the inspiration from his lofty heights, Hans Posse had been the dynamo that ran it. Until Wolffhardt's appointment as Director of the Linz library, he had been responsible for everything, spending over 20,000,000 reichsmarks on purchases for Linz. His death left a vast gap that was not to be easily filled, making Hitler realize how much he had depended on this one man. For weeks he hesitated over his successor, slowly coming to the conclusion that there was no one man who could fill Posse's shoes, who possessed to the same degree his knowledge of art, energy, and organizing ability. The rivalry amongst the possible candidates grew intense as every museum director in Germany tried to catch the Fuehrer's eye. Those in Vienna claimed they were the best men for the job, and loudly advertised their qualities. For nearly three months after Posse's funeral the Sonderauftrag was like a chicken running round without its head.

Hitler finally solved the problem by making a surprise appointment and reorganizing the chain of command so as to split up Posse's duties. On 22 March 1943, Dr Lammers in Berlin issued a directive to all commanders in the occupied countries:

After the death of Dr Posse, the Fuehrer has assigned to the provisional director of the Dresden Art Gallery, Dr Voss, the duty of preparing the decisions on whether the Fuehrer's right re the disposition of art collections and works of art should be exercised.

I request you therefore, if the occasion arises, to communicate with Dr Voss.

It was as if a 100–1 shot had romped home in the Derby. Hermann Voss was not a party member and was well-known for his lack of enthusiasm towards his Nazi leaders. Since 1935 he had been the unpaid director of the Wiesbaden Gallery, moving to Dresden after Posse's death. Previously he had not even been considered as a runner in the Linz Stakes, now he had been placed overnight in a position of considerable power. Goebbels informed him of his appointment and he was summoned to Hitler's presence to discuss future plans for the Linz museum. In art circles his appointment was a major sensation, made possible because it was dependent solely on the whims of one man.

Hitler had recognized from the beginning that his choice was not another Hans Posse. Hermann Voss was informed that he would be in charge solely of the Fuehrermuseum, though it was emphasized that paintings would always be the dominant feature of the Linz collections. Dr Wolffhardt already possessed equal authority but now greater powers were given to Dr Ruprecht and Dr Dworschak to run the armour and coin collections respectively. They also had a new superior in place of Dr Posse—Dr Helmut von Hummel, Bormann's new secretary.

Von Hummel had succeeded Dr Hanssen in October 1942. He had engineered and gained much greater powers, which were reinforced when he was given a direct position in the Linz chain of command. Aged nearly forty, of medium height and build, and with a prominent sword scar on his left cheek, von Hummel operated from three offices. He worked at the Fuehrerbau in Munich's Koenigsplatz (now renamed Meiserstrasse), had another office at Berchtesgaden, and a third in the special office for high party officials at 16 Prinzregentenplatz in Munich. He also worked at his home, a villa at Mendess, Upper Danube. Once his new appointment was announced, von Hummel became extremely active in Linz affairs. He inspected new acquisitions in Paris, visited the repositories in the South Tyrol, and took an active part in the negotiations for the large collections that were being forced on to the market because of their owners' need for the basic necessities of life.

Both Ruprecht and Dworschak welcomed the greater powers bestowed upon them. They were ambitious men with high opinions of their skill in their own fields. They got on well with von Hummel because though he was in charge on administrative matters, he never set himself up as an expert in either armour or rare coins. These matters he left to the experts, for which both Ruprecht and Dworschak were grateful. Though the directive formally to establish a coin collection at Linz had been issued by Hitler only six months previously, Dworschak was already employing a staff of five coin experts, all of whom had their salaries paid direct from Berchtesgaden. As for Ruprecht, he now found himself being consulted on the plans being drawn up for the armour museum.

Voss's appointment inevitably meant changes in the Sonderauftrag's personnel. There was also an upheaval in the relationships of the various art dealers, men of the stature of Karl Haberstock finding themselves out in the cold. But one man whose position was greatly strengthened was Gottfried Reimer. Voss recognized how much he needed his knowledge and experience if he was to take control without running into too many snags, but finding he got on well with this quiet young man, he permitted Reimer to take over more of the administrative work, including most of the personal contacts with the Nazi leaders which Voss was glad to evade. Later Reimer was placed in sole charge of the tremendous task of supervising the thousands of works of art moved to the Alt Aussee salt-mine as the Allied aerial bombing of Germany increased its intensity.

Voss did not get on well with Dr Rudolf Oertel, another Linz administrator whom he had known before the war in Florence. From Italy Oertel, also aged forty, had joined Posse in Dresden, and after the latter's funeral he had run the Sonderauftrag jointly with Reimer until Voss's appointment. Oertel wrote an article in commemoration of Posse which was published in *Das Reich* early in 1943. Voss's dislike of Oertel was based largely on the latter's aggressive pro-Nazi sympathies. He did not feel strong enough to force a showdown, permitting him to stay on in the administration but with reduced powers. Voss shed no tears when Oertel was called up in 1944 and vanished in the direction of the Russian front.

For others, Voss's appointment meant advancement. Dr Franz Schubert, an assistant at the Dresden Kupferstich Kabinett, had been switched to cataloguing Linz drawings and prints. Now Voss promoted him to be in charge of the Schloss Weesenstein repository, about twelve miles from Dresden, the biggest storehouse used by Hitler until the bulk of the Linz collection was moved into the Alt Aussee salt-mine. Schubert held this position until 1944, when he was called up for military service. He was succeeded by Dr Hans Helmut Klihm, who had previously worked with Dr Walter Bornheim, director of the Galerie fuer Alte Kunst, in Munich. Klihm's appointment was proof that Voss had the courage not to permit political considerations to influence his decisions. Aged twenty-seven and a graduate of Munich University, Klihm was the son of a lawyer boycotted by the Nazis for defending Jews in the courts.

Amongst the accredited Linz dealers, the new figure of power to emerge was Dr Hildebrandt Gurlitt, a friend of Voss, and the first recipient of a Linz certificate who was part-Jewish.

Like Voss, Gurlitt had the reputation of being anti-Nazi. His grandmother was Jewish and his father the famous architectural historian Cornelius Gurlitt. Born in 1895, Hildebrandt Gurlitt had first become museum director at Zwickau and later Hamburg, but the Nazis had marked him down and as early as 1931 their growing influence was sufficient to cut short his career. Gurlitt decided to become an art dealer in Hamburg and often put on exhibitions of those artists whose paintings were described as not being in sympathy with National Socialist philosophy. It was not only a gesture of defiance but also an expression of Gurlitt's admiration for the Impressionists.

Somehow managing to steer clear of further trouble, Gurlitt

moved to Dresden in 1942. Voss repaid his friendship by making him accredited buyer in Paris, an important appointment because events elsewhere had created a power vacuum in this vitally important market.

Always a man with a long memory, Martin Bormann had never forgiven Rosenberg for siding with Goering in outwitting the Fuehrer. Bormann had no proof but was prepared to act on his strong suspicions. He was well aware that Rosenberg had firmly hitched his wagon to Goering's star but now that star was in the descendant after the failure of the Luftwaffe over Britain, in the Western Desert and the Mediterranean, and on the Russian front. In April 1943, one month after Voss's appointment, Bormann decided it was time to act, judging correctly that Goering would be too occupied in trying to stop himself going down the slide to utter protests on behalf of a mere henchman. Bormann obtained Hitler's agreement to the breaking-up of the Einsatzstab Rosenberg on the grounds that its functions were now superfluous.

On 21 April Bormann wrote to Rosenberg who, already seeing the writing on the wall, had left Paris to live at 17 Margaretenstrasse in Berlin. Though addressing him as 'very honourable Party Comrade Rosenberg', Bormann's letter was curt and to the point:

The Fuehrer wished that the art objects seized by your staff be transferred as soon as possible to the Fuehrer's experts for further handling. Expert for the projected Linz Library is Dr Friedrich Wolffhardt, Fuehrerbau, Munich. Expert for the Linz galleries which the Fuehrer is considering is Professor Dr Voss, Dresden State Art Gallery. Expert for the remaining collections which the Fuehrer wishes to build in Linz at the present time is Dr von Hummel, Fuehrerbau, Munich.

Heil Hitler!

No vote of thanks, no best wishes for the future. A man of Rosenberg's stature could not have been dismissed in colder terms and it must have been a letter that gave Bormann great satisfaction to write. He had waited two years to deliver it, knowing that Hitler would not thank him if he started an open conflict with the powerful Hermann Goering at a time when the Reich Marshal was so popular. But those days were gone, and the great men behind the scenes were taking over.

Rosenberg, a member of the Nazi Party since 1919, became notorious as an arch-hater of the Jews. With him, it was a pathological condition, and it is of some irony that he was succeeded as the chief Linz buyer in Paris by a man who was part-Jewish and had suffered at the hands of the Nazi Party because of his race. Armed with his Linz certificate, Dr Gurlitt arrived in Paris. The years had taught him caution and he stayed away from official Nazi circles. He carried out most of his transactions through Theo Hermssen, jnr., a Dutch art dealer residing at the Hotel de Jersey in the Rue de la Grange-Batelière.

Gurlitt spent freely in Paris. He was forced to because prices had risen steadily throughout the war. He paid 2,200,000 reichsmarks for four Beauvais tapestries which he sold to Linz. He also bought a pair of mythological scenes by Crespi and from the dealer Gustav Rochlitz acquired such paintings as an Italian harbour scene by the eighteenth-century French painter, Joseph Vernet (450,000 francs); 'Young Man with a Cat' by Molenaer (400,000 francs); a battle-scene by the German painter Januarius Zick (200,000 francs) which must have been much to Hitler's liking; and a landscape by Jan Keirinx (100,000 francs).

The most important painting purchased by Gurlitt, in his own estimation, was turned down by Voss. This was a male portrait attributed to the fifteenth-century French painter Jean Fouquet, first and greatest of the Loire school. Gurlitt, who claimed that he never bought a painting unless it was freely offered for sale, was so enthusiastic when he heard about this picture that he made a special trip to Marseilles to see its owner, Count Demandolx. They agreed on a price of 800,000 reichsmarks (16,000,000 francs) and Gurlitt gave the Count personally more than half the sum, paying the rest through Hermssen in Paris. An export order was made out by Michel Martin, an assistant in the Department of Paintings at the Louvre, and the picture was transported to Dresden. But Voss refused to buy it, doubting its authenticity, and Gurlitt eventually sold it to the Wallraf-Richartz museum in Cologne.

Gurlitt seldom bought from private collectors, preferring to confine his activities to the established dealers. At the end of the war twenty boxes filled with paintings were found amongst his possessions, most of them bought in Paris or Amsterdam. He had no established commission for his Linz sales, including his profit in the asked price. Once he had accepted a picture, Voss rarely quibbled about the price, telling Gurlitt that there was plenty of money and there was no reason why it shouldn't be spent. With prices still spiralling upwards, this wasn't difficult despite the shrinking market. In the years before the war Gurlitt considered himself fortunate if his annual income reached 45,000 reichsmarks, but in his first year as a Linz agent his income rose steeply to over 200,000 reichsmarks. Few other men at one time persecuted by the Nazis because of their Jewish background later made so much money out of their Fuehrer.

In the massive raid on Dresden Gurlitt and his family escaped injury but their home was destroyed. When the war ended, the Allied authorities found them at the home of Baron von Poellnitz where Karl Haberstock was sheltering. The Baron's Aschbach estate seemed to have become a general refuge for bombed-out Linz agents.

*

Hermann Voss estimated that he had three main agents: Hildebrandt Gurlitt, Dr Erhard Goepel who was still the chief Linz buyer in Holland, and Dr Herbst who bought extensively in Holland and Paris. Formerly a member of the staff of the Dorotheum in Vienna and speaking with a strong Viennese accent, Herbst was appointed a Linz agent by Voss and bought over 250 paintings in Holland alone. In 1943 he made several buying trips to Paris and also made several purchases in Brussels through the dealer Maurice Lagrand.

Almost as important as the top three men was a dealer called

Georg Schilling—another Voss appointment—who had a gallery at 39 Kommodienstrasse in Cologne. Though German-born he lived with his Swiss wife in Zurich, but frequently travelled throughout Europe. In Brussels he bought a work by the Flemish painter Jacob Jordaens, entitled 'Presentation of the Virgin in the Temple', which Reger later entered as Linz Item 3444. Before Voss took him up, Schilling negotiated Goering's purchase of the collection owned by Madame van Gelder, receiving 10% of the 220,000 reischmarks paid for it.

Voss used his power to issue Linz certificates as a means of helping his friends. One was Walter Weber, a wealthy Bonn collector, who first met Voss in London when the latter was still at Wiesbaden. Later Weber objected to the Nazification of the Bonn museum and willed his collection to Wiesbaden, Voss taking them to Dresden for safekeeping and later storing them in the Schloss Weesenstein. Because Weber wished to live in Paris, Voss made him a Linz buyer, though he was able to sell only six minor paintings to Linz, the Nazi authorities refusing to grant him export licences for his other purchases. Voss also made Gustav Rochlitz a Linz buyer solely to keep him out of the Army, subsequently buying only four paintings from him. These included a Madonna by the Florentine painter Piero di Cosimo, and a Droogsloot with the odd title, 'Landscape with a Sick Person at a Fish Pond'.

Another important Linz agent was Hans Lange, Director of the Berlin auction-house that bears his name. When he was conscripted into the Luftwaffe, Lange pulled strings to get himself appointed courier with duties that often meant journeys to Paris. In this way he was able to buy paintings for Linz as a profitable sideline. These included a large painting by Hubert Robert for which he paid 175,000 reichsmarks—a huge sum to be laid out by a mere Luftwaffe courier—which he resold to Maria Dietrich for a fat profit. She in turn made more money out of it when selling it to Linz and Reger solemnly entered it under the title, 'Classical Landscape with Roman Soldiers and a Woman with a Child in front of a Ruined Monument'. As the Robert covered thirty square feet of canvas, Reger felt his verboseness was justified. Hans Lange also sold to Linz a Renaissance tapestry and two Liotard still-lifes that were enthusiastically recommended by Bruno Lohse.

Voss made a number of purchases from Bornheim. Made in August 1943, these included a male portrait by Bartel Bruyn and drawings by Baudoin, Boucher, Tiepolo, and Watteau, but Bornheim's most important sale to Linz had been made five years earlier. This was Botticelli's 'Simonetta', entered in the Linz records as Item 743 but which in 1938 was held in a Berlin bank as part of the Kappel collection. A representative of the bank telephoned Bornheim, who saw the painting and offered 100,000 reichsmarks spot cash, and a further 150,000 to be paid later. This was accepted and Bornheim went to Hitler, who agreed to buy the painting, subject to its being examined and declared genuine by Ernst Buchner, Director of the Bavarian State Museums. But Buchner refused even to look at the painting, saying that he knew it well and that it was too greatly restored to be worth much money.

When Hitler heard this, he refused to buy the Botticelli. Bornheim was so furious that he took the painting to Cologne and Vienna, where it was X-rayed and examined by experts. He was able to return to Munich with sworn statements by the most respected art experts that the only restoration to the painting was a single narrow crack which had been filled in and repainted. Shown these documents, Hitler changed his mind and bought the Botticelli for 300,000 reichsmarks, giving Bornheim a profit of 50,000. Only later did he discover that Buchner, Karl Haberstock, and a well-known Munich dealer, named Boehler, had formed a triumvirate with the aim of buying the painting at a low price by pretending that it was not in good condition. They might have succeeded if the bank had not contacted Bornheim, who had acted on and trusted his own judgement.

This incident did not discredit Buchner in Hitler's eyes. He was often employed by the Linz administration as a consultative expert, and he sold to Linz four mythological scenes by Carl Rahl which he purchased from a private collection in Austria. He also approved the sale to Linz of fifteen paintings, including two Makarts, from the collection of the Bavarian State Gallery. The total price was 195,000 reichsmarks.

The numerous dealers selling to Linz were tributaries flowing into a mainstream controlled by Hermann Voss. When he took over the Linz collection, he faced a seller's market, as an army of dealers fought each other for almost every painting that came up for sale. To make sure the Fuehrer got the best of what was available, money had to be spent lavishly and Voss did not hesitate to do so. If he lacked the visionary zeal of Hans Posse, he could still enjoy a buying spree as much as the next man, particularly when the money wasn't his own. To some degree he sacrificed quality for quantity, making purchases that would never have been negotiated by his predecessor. In the twelve months prior to his appointment only 122 paintings were bought for the Linz collection but each had been carefully chosen by Dr Posse. After his first twelve months as Director, Voss could report that he had purchased 878 paintings. On 15 April 1944 he gave the details in a letter to Bormann, itemizing them as follows:

    45 German paintings before 1800
   142 German paintings after 1800
    30 Netherlands school before 1600
    88 17th and 18th century Flemish
   395 17th and 18th century Dutch
    54 19th century Dutch
    72 Italian
    42 French
     5 Spanish
     5 English

In addition, Voss reported to Bormann that he had also acquired for Linz 136 drawings and watercolours; 174 prints, including the complete graphic works of Marius Bauer and Otto Greiner; eight pastels and miniatures; ten sculptures; and thirty-nine *objets d'art* and furniture. Voss was obviously the main source of paintings for Linz but others did reach Hans Reger in the Fuehrerbau, most of them presents to Hitler which he had forwarded on.

Until his appointment to Linz Voss had possessed the reputation for being anti-Nazi but now it seemed he thought it only proper to express his appreciation to Hitler for choosing him to fill a position of such power and responsibility. As his annual report on Linz was sent to Bormann only five days before Hitler's birthday, Voss decided to include with it a present to the Fuehrer with which he sent a fulsome covering letter to Bormann. Voss wrote:

May I ask you to have the great kindness to present to the Fuehrer on the occasion of his birthday, and with the sincerest wishes of myself and my colleagues and the expression of our deepest gratitude, the accompanying two cases, which contain a precious Greek gold head-band of the 5th century B.C., and a Greek silver wreath with gold leaves, and a gold medallion decorated with a Sinesus head of the same period.

Both wreaths, which we were able to acquire from former private German collections in Darmstadt, have been painstakingly restored to their pristine beauty over a period of months by the restorer of the State Treasure Room in Dresden.

At the same time permit me to offer you another album of new acquisitions of paintings, as a review of the year's purchases from 1 April 1943 to 31 March 1944 which I have made for the Linz Art Museum, and especially for the Linz Painting Gallery.

Heil Hitler!

This ingratiating letter no doubt had the desired effect on Hitler's overweening vanity. But it was somewhat tactless to present the Fuehrer with a gold wreath of leaves, the symbol of the victor, at a time when he was facing defeat on all fronts and rapidly losing the war. Moreover, examination of the Linz records later showed that this Greek jewellery was entered by Reger as Linz Item 948, overwhelming evidence that it had been obtained for the collection long before Voss appeared on the scene. He had dug up something purchased by Hans Posse, got it refurbished and then presented it to the Fuehrer with his undying devotion. But, as usual with Hitler, the apple polishing worked. Voss was able to see the war out without being sacked or disgraced, even in those last insane days when the Fuehrer had Goering arrested and no man could consider himself safe.

*

One single purchase which increased Voss's first year total by 262 items was the major part of the Schloss collection, the second largest obtained by Hitler and exceeded only by that of the Rothschilds.

The exact number of paintings owned by the Schloss family was 333, most of them by Dutch masters. At the outbreak of war they had been hidden in the South of France, which later became Vichy territory, and by 1943, despite several attempts, the collection remained one of the very few of substantial size to evade seizure by the Nazis in one way or another. Posse knew of the collection, as did most experts, and was interested in acquiring it, but he took no definite steps to do so, mainly because there was so much else on the market and he hadn't the time to track down its whereabouts. He had discussed the collection with Hitler but no positive decisions were arrived at. The matter just rested.

Then Karl Haberstock visited Nice on a business trip. He stayed at the Hotel Negresco where one evening he had an unexpected visitor. A woman arrived unannounced, said she was related to the Schloss family and understood he was an art dealer. Would he, she asked, be interested in buying the entire collection? Then she added that he could not see it as it was hidden away, but if he was prepared to make a satisfactory offer, and it would have to be substantial, a sale might be arranged. She showed Haberstock a typewritten list of the paintings, describing them briefly, but there were no illustrations or anything resembling a catalogue. Haberstock told her shortly that he never bought a picture without seeing it first; only if that could be arranged would he be prepared to do business. The woman took back her list and went away.

If she had not achieved an offer, she had at least aroused the old man's interest. He returned to Paris to seek out the two men greatly in his debt—Roger Dequoy and his associate, Georges Destrem, who owed Haberstock a favour since he had used his influence to free Destrem's stepson who was a prisoner of war. Haberstock suggested to the two men that they acted as his agents in trying to trace the Schloss collection and then used the information as a lever towards buying it at a reasonable price. Both the Frenchmen instantly agreed, not only because they were in Haberstock's debt, but also because they appreciated the extremely fat commission that would be their due if they were successful.

Both Dequoy and Destrem put out strong feelers amongst their contacts in French art circles. In August 1942 Dequoy wrote to Haberstock: 'I am at present negotiating the Schloss affair and am about to see one of the heirs in Grenoble.' Later Dequoy reported that he had been told that the heirs to the collection had left France, and a further report from Destrem stated that he understood that the collection was definitely up for sale. This last brought an immediate reply from Haberstock:

> If I understood you, the heirs are in need of money and might wish to sell some of the items. . . . I would very much like to know from what source you have learned that they wish to sell. How will you succeed in finding the pictures? I should very much like to acquire some items of the collection, or even the whole collection, if possible. Try to succeed. . . .

In the same letter Haberstock hinted that others were also seeking the collection and cautiously added that he would only pay commission to the person who actually obtained the paintings. Replying a week later, Destrem reported that a lawyer who had spoken to him about the collection was temporarily away from Paris. As soon as he returned he would be seen and the results reported to Haberstock.

Dequoy and Destrem were not in need of any encouragement. But though they were seeing a great many people, they were making little headway. Several informants swore they knew where the collection was and promised to take them to it but nothing ever materialized. Meanwhile Haberstock's hints that others were interested were proving all too true. In a shrinking art market, Hitler decided that the Schloss collection would make a valuable addition to Linz. He gave instructions for strong pressure to be put on the Vichy Government to find out where the paintings were, confiscate them and bring them to Paris.

Pierre Laval needed little persuading. Only too eager to help, he ordered Abel Bonnard, Vichy Minister of Education and Darquier de Pellepoix, French Commissioner for Jewish Affairs, to take the necessary steps. De Pellepoix called in an art dealer named Lefranc, appointed him Vichy administrator to the Schloss collection, and gave him certain instructions.

Lefranc and three other Vichy officials travelled to Nice. There they arrested Henri Schloss and his wife, informing them that they were acting on the instructions of Pierre Laval. It did not take them long to learn the whereabouts of the collection but now arose the difficult problem of transporting it through Vichy France to Paris, a hazardous business in view of the growing strength of the French Resistance. De Pellepoix remembered that in the halcyon days of the Einsatzstab Rosenberg, Goering had never hesitated to use his Luftwaffe to escort art treasures, particularly when they were bound for Karinhall, and he Pellepoix decided to enlist Goering's aid again.

He arranged a meeting in Paris with Bruno Lohse, Goering's agent, and introduced him to Lefranc, explaining that he was the authorized agent for the Schloss collection. De Pellepoix informed Lohse that he had been instructed to sell the Schloss collection which was now in the hands of his Government but in order to minimize adverse public opinion, six preliminary conditions of sale had to be observed:

1. The collection was not to be confiscated by German officers once it reached Paris.

2. There was to be no obligation to complete a sale once the pictures were in Paris.

3. Assurances must be given that the collection could be returned at any time to unoccupied territory.

4. Transportation to Paris was to be undertaken by the German Government.

5. The collection was to be placed in the Dreyfus Bank in Paris under full French control.

6. The Louvre authorities were to see the collection first in order to exercise their legal right to a first option on any part.

Lohse communicated these conditions to Goering, whose collector's interest in the size of the Schloss was sufficiently aroused to make him agree to them without reservations. It was arranged that the paintings, packed in seven large cases, should be handed over at the little town of Tulle, near Limoges.

Goering was now faced with the difficult problem of transportation. He could order half the Luftwaffe to protect it while it travelled through Occupied France but Vichy country was a different matter. In the end he decided to hire a large truck in Paris, recruit a tough civilian escort who were promised high pay, and instruct a security official to go along to make all the explanations if they were stopped travelling through Unoccupied France. Before leaving, the security man was told this was a French affair, being carried out on behalf of the Vichy Government, and he was just going along for the ride.

The truck reached Tulle without being stopped by anyone. The seven cases of paintings were there but Lefranc and other Vichy officials had failed to turn up to hand them over officially. Tired of waiting, the men with the truck loaded the cases and drove off, eager to get back to Paris and the money that was waiting for them. They were barely outside Tulle when they were stopped by a strong force of local French police who had not been told what was going on. A tremendous argument, beloved by all Frenchmen, ensued at a machine-gun rate of speech and the security man was able to slip away unnoticed to telephone security headquarters at Limoges, asking for help. An armed security guard arrived, joined in the argument and then ended it by taking the cases to their barracks in Limoges after declaring that they would only hold them until the question of their ownership had been decided.

Frantic telephone calls now followed in all directions, one being made to Bruno Lohse in Paris. He at once telephoned Goering in Berlin, who groaned audibly and then ordered that there must be no delay in shifting the paintings from the security barracks to some place where they were under French control. This was done by moving them to a local bank. Further negotiations followed, and as a result de Pellepoix was at last able to bring the Schloss collection to Paris. As agreed, the seven large crates were placed in the Dreyfus Bank.

But the damage had been done. Word went round that it was the Germans who had confiscated the collection which they had kept in their barracks before finally condescending to hand it over to the Vichy authorities. Goering decided that this was a wasps' nest that mustn't sting him and declared that he was no longer interested in buying the collection. The time was October 1943, when his fortunes were on the ebb, and he wasn't risking further trouble. He also realized that he didn't have sufficient money, some experts already saying that the Schloss collection was worth at least fifty million francs.

But if Goering wasn't interested, another German in Paris was. Dr Erhard Goepel, chief Linz buyer in Holland, often visited Paris to see what paintings he could buy, and he was particularly interested in the Schloss collection because of the large number of Dutch masterpieces it contained. Voss had tried to make him confine his activities to Holland as he was treading on Hildebrandt Gurlitt's toes but without any success. Voss felt he still wasn't secure enough in the job to force a showdown.

As soon as the Schloss collection had arrived, Goepel sent an urgent message to Voss, suggesting that Linz should obtain as much of the collection as possible. He telephoned Voss, wrote to him and finally visited him in Dresden. By now aware that the purchase would be a feather in his cap Voss agreed, stipulating that the dealings must be carried out through the German Embassy in Paris to ensure that no trouble broke out with the French. Negotiations began in which the six conditions made known to Goering were reiterated. Finally it was agreed that the Louvre should have first choice and the Sonderauftrag Linz have the right to buy all the remainder at prices agreed by experts appointed by the Vichy Government. As the man on the spot, Goepel was given full authority by Voss to select those paintings suitable for Linz.

Dr Gerlach, counsellor to the German Embassy, took it upon himself to ensure that the six conditions of sale were strictly observed. At the Dreyfus Bank the paintings were opened by French officials without any Germans being present. The Louvre's experts went through them and decided to buy forty-nine at a stipulated price of 18,975,000 francs. This money, it was said, would go to the Schloss family, who were being given no say in how much their own property was worth.

Several days later Dr Goepel visited the collection, accompanied by Bruno Lohse, Lefranc, and Cornelius Postma, the Dutch dealer appointed as official appraiser by the Vichy Government. After considerable consideration and haggling, it was agreed that Linz should buy 262 paintings for the round sum of fifty million francs. The papers were signed, the pictures taken to the Jeu de Paume museum before being transported to Germany. They arrived at the Fuehrerbau in Munich where Voss examined them but made no changes in Goepel's selection. After being catalogued by Reger, they were moved down to the basement air-raid shelters.

If Voss believed that words of praise were on their way from the Fuehrer, he was to be quickly disillusioned. He learned from Reger that Hitler was furious because the Louvre had been allowed to buy the best of the collection and he, Adolf Hitler, given what was left over. Voss also learned that Heinrich Hoffmann had been telling the Fuehrer that the paintings bought by Goepel were far below the standard of the rest of the Linz collection. It was little wonder that Voss decided the time was ripe to ingratiate himself with Hitler through a birthday present of Grecian laurel leaves.

The Schloss family was betrayed utterly. The Vichy Government never paid up the promised 18,975,000 francs, the price of the Louvre's forty-nine paintings. As for Hitler, he promptly paid his fifty million francs but that went not to the Schloss family but into the coffers of de Pellepoix's anti-Semitic organization.

When the confiscation had been carried out the Vichy Government gave an assurance that any paintings left unsold would be returned to the family. After the Louvre and Hitler had made their purchases, there were still twenty-two canvases left over. Instead of being returned, they were offered to favoured art dealers by Lefranc at give-away prices. Goepel bought Rembrandt's 'Jew in a Fur Hat', which he sold to Linz, as well as a religious fragment attributed to Roger van der Weyden. Two other small portraits, attributed to Rembrandt and Frans Hals, also found their way into Hitler's possession. Prices charged by Lefranc included 10,000 francs for a Rembrandt, 2,000 francs each for two Guardis, 25,000 francs for a Rubens, 30,000 francs for a Frans Hals, and as little as 100 francs for a painting attributed to the Dutch master, Adriaen Brouwer. It depicted a man searching his person for lice and was later sold for 300,000 francs. Another of these paintings was Duyster's 'Couple Reading a Letter', listed by Lefranc at 10,000 francs, equal to 500 reichsmarks. The buyer sold it to Frau Maria Dietrich for 12,500 reichsmarks, who in turn found a German collector willing to pay 18,500 reichsmarks.

The 262 paintings of the Schloss collection were entered in the records as Linz Item 3108, all coming under the same number. They represented the worst possible example of a forced sale, engineered by the Germans with the willing co-operation of a pusillanimous and equally ruthless Vichy Government. And by treacherously betraying their promises, Vichy had managed to satisfy German pressure and make a profit of fifty million francs into the bargain.

CHAPTER NINE

Burying the Treasure

By the early part of 1944 Hitler had accumulated such a vast number of works of art for Linz that the crowded shelters in the Fuehrerbau could take no more, and the overflow was going out into a number of storehouses elsewhere. The three most important of these was the Schloss Thuerntal near Krems-muenster, the Hohenfurth monastery just inside the Czech border and the Schloss Neuschwanstein near Fuessen.

In the shelters of the Fuehrerbau wooden shelves had been installed to hold paintings packed in large crates, but though as many as possible were crammed in, it was obvious as early as the summer of 1941 that other storage space would have to be found. The first place chosen as a Linz repository was the Schloss Thuerntal, and for more than two years it received a steady flow of art treasures from Munich. Hans Reger's records showed these consignments:

1 August 1941—120 paintings; 15 August 1941—184 paint-ings; 29 August 1941—149 paintings; 12 September 1941—175 paintings and other items; 17 October 1941—166 paint-ings and other items; 18 September 1942—110 paintings and other items; 16 October 1942—174 paintings and other items; 20 May 1943—140 paintings and other items; 30 June 1943—109 paintings and other items; 20 August 1943—141 paint-

ings and other items; 13 November 1943—90 paintings and other items; and 28 November 1943—174 paintings and other items.

These dispatches were made by trucks under military escort, a total of 1,732 paintings plus *objets d'art*, tapestries, and other art treasures. In its turn the Schloss Thuerntal became filled to capacity and Reger had to look elsewhere. The Hohenfurth monastery had been used solely for storing stone sculpture and ironwork but on 6 March 1944 Reger was forced to send there a consignment of 42 paintings.

The Schloss Neuschwanstein was the main storehouse of the Einsatzstab Rosenberg. As Goering had already wangled what he wanted for Karinhall, Hitler had first choice of everything stored in the Schloss, a Gothic nightmarish castle in the air, built by Mad King Ludwig of Bavaria. Except for a few rooms in the state apartments, the entire castle was crammed with art treasures—paintings, tapestries, ornaments, and antique pieces, stored on endless wooden racks. Two large chests contained fabulous Rothschild *objets d'art* and also in the castle were more than a thousand pieces of silver from the David-Weill collection. Perhaps the outstanding painting amongst thousands was Rubens's 'Three Graces', seized from Meurice de Rothschild.

The two biggest single deliveries to Neuschwanstein were made in April 1941, when thirty full goods trucks arrived, and in the following October when a further twenty-three arrived. By 1944 the records kept in the castle showed the massive total of 21,903 works of art from 203 private collections, nearly all of them Jewish. Much of this collection had been photographed and there were more than 8,000 negatives, the prints of most of them having already been shown to Hitler. The intake of items dried up with the dismantling of the Einsatzstab on Bormann's orders, leaving Neuschwanstein a static Aladdin's Cave, waiting to be divided amongst the Nazi leaders when the war was won, with Hitler very definitely at the head of the queue.

By the spring of 1944 round-the-clock bombing of Germany had been fully mounted by the Allies. Planes of the Royal Air Force came by the hundreds at night and during the day

American Flying Fortresses with their bristling guns continued the bombardment. It was not long before Hitler decided that most of his storehouses, including the Fuehrerbau, were no longer safe from attack. He ordered the removal of his vast booty to mines deep underground, in remote areas which were of negligible military importance.

The evacuation was not confined to works of art. One hundred tons of gold bullion from Germany's accumulated gold reserves plus a number of national art treasures that had belonged to Kaiser Friedrich were taken to the Merkers salt-mine, situated ninety miles west of Weimar, and buried 2,100 feet underground. When the Allied armies swept across Germany, this was the first important hiding-place of Nazi treasure to be discovered, and then only by the sheerest good fortune Two American military policemen patrolling the area stopped two German women who were seeking a local midwife. The soldiers were helpful and courteous, and the women so grateful that they told them they believed 'something' was buried in the Merkers salt-mine. An exploration-party went down and found the gold, the first hint to the Allies that other salt-mines, ideal because of their constant humidity, might be the key to the mystery of where Hitler and other Nazi leaders had hidden the art treasures they had looted from every part of Europe.

In a Munich still in German hands, Hans Reger was given the task of moving the huge collection of Linz items in the Fuehrerbau's shelters to the salt-mines at Alt Aussee, chosen by Hitler as his main last-ditch hiding-place for his collection. Gottfried Reimer was placed in charge of the salt-mine, taking delivery of each consignment and burying the art treasures deep underground. The route between Munich and Alt Aussee consisted of tortuous roads through the mountains and the conscientious Reger insisted on travelling with each convoy to satisfy himself that it had arrived safely. For Reger, borne down by the responsibility of moving great masterpieces that were part of Europe's heritage as well as being enormously valuable, each trip must have been a nightmare as the heavy lorries travelled round hairpin bends and up and down formidably steep gradients with sheer drops a few feet away. No accidents

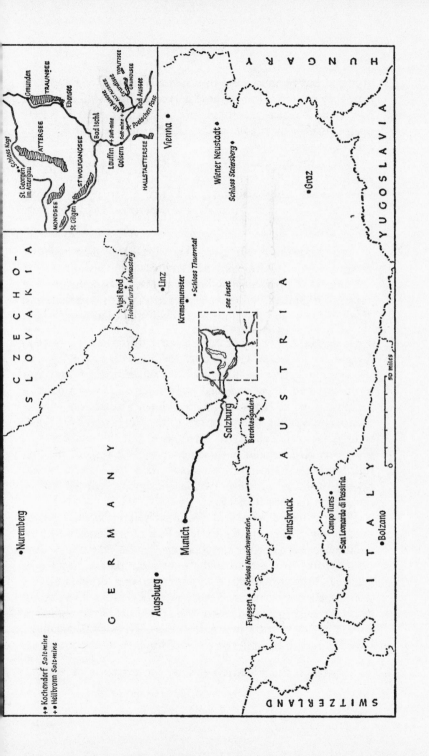

occurred but he must have breathed a huge sigh of relief each time they arrived. During those nerve-racking months he must have come to realize that these were only panic measures, merely postponing the inevitable, as the Allied armies and the Russians bit deeper into Europe.

During the months of May and October 1944 Reger shifted the bulk of 1,788 art treasures from the Fuehrerbau. These consisted of 1,687 paintings and 101 other items, mainly sculptures, *objets d'art*, mosaics, and tapestries. Deliveries were made on these dates:

19 May—248 paintings; 24 June—200 paintings; 15 August—262 paintings; 24 August—203 paintings; 31 August—163 paintings and other items; 13 September—133 paintings and other items; 21 September—91 paintings and other items; and 4 October—249 paintings and other items.

On 23 November Reger made a hurried trip to Alt Aussee to discuss the situation with Reimer, taking with him a few odd paintings and other small items. They talked about future consignments and Reger returned to Munich to face a mounting backlog of work. Hitler was closing down a number of smaller caches and sending their contents to the Fuehrerbau for Reger to organize their delivery to Alt Aussee. But the intake was so great that Reger could not keep pace with it despite working long hours every day. He was so busy receiving Linz items that he was unable to organize another consignment to Alt Aussee during the remainder of 1944.

The year 1945 dawned with Germany's defeat looming nearer as each day passed. On the Eastern Front her armies were now reeling backwards before the Russians. In the West the Ardennes offensive had proved to be only a temporary respite. In January Hitler, whose madness was increasing, decided that he would make an inventory of every work of art in his possession, either confiscated or purchased. If he could not take it with him, at least he would know how much it was. Through Bormann he issued orders to Himmler as Chief of the S.S. on the 26th:

Based on the Fuehrer's orders, the existence of all con-

fiscated works of art, especially paintings, objects of artistic
interest and weapons of artistic importance, in Greater Germany and the Occupied Territories is to be reported to the
Fuehrer's advisers in such matters, who, on consideration of
the individual cases, will sent a report to the Fuehrer through
me so that the Fuehrer can himself decide what use he will
make of the acquired articles.

This ruling must be strictly upheld by all branches of the
S.S.

Thus, as his dream of a Nazi-dominated Europe crumbled
into dust, Hitler was going to select the great works of art that
would go into the Linz museums, now never to be built, to
glorify his memory that was now bedraggled by defeat. It was an
action comparable with Nero's fiddling while Rome burned.

The order listed his four advisers:

For paintings and sculpture: Professor Dr Voss (State
Gallery of Painting, Dresden).

For weapons of artistic importance: Professor Dr Ruprecht
(Vienna, Neue Berg).

For coins and medals: Director Dr Dworschak (Vienna,
Kunsthistorisches Museum).

For books and written material: Dr Wolffhardt (Grundlsee,
Upper Danube).

These further orders from Hitler weighed heavily on Hans
Reger. He was faced with making a detailed inventory of every
work of art still remaining in the basement of the Fuehrerbau
after months of numerous deliveries and consignments to Alt
Aussee. He started this huge task on 1 February, even as more
paintings and sculpture designated for Linz arrived to be
numbered and catalogued. As he strove to keep his records in
order Reger gave up any idea of organizing further convoys to
Alt Aussee. He was far from comforted by reports that the
records at the salt-mine were in chaos because Reimer had not
been able to keep pace with the intake. As Germany faced defeat, her proverbial efficiency was fast disintegrating.

By early April the fate of Munich was sealed as American troops swept through Southern Germany, meeting only sporadic resistance. On 13 April, as an act of desperation, Reger sent a last consignment of 137 paintings to Alt Aussee, the only one to leave the Fuehrerbau during 1945. This time he did not travel with it, being unable to spare the time away from his records. On 29 April, when the first troops of the American Seventh Army entered the city, there were still 723 works of art stored in the Fuehrerbau, including the entire Schloss collection of 262 paintings. On the same day Reger decided it would be wiser if he left for Alt Aussee. As the last civilian remaining in the building, he handed over the keys to Captain von Xylander, commander of the military unit defending the Fuehrerbau, got into his car and started on his twelfth trip to the salt-mine. But this time he did not get very far, being stopped some miles east of Munich by an S.S. detachment who were singularly unimpressed when he produced documents proving that he was employed directly by the Fuehrer. They restrained themselves from harming him but rudely took his car, leaving Reger to trudge wearily back to Munich, where he sought the haven of his apartment at 7 Gaibelstrasse.

On the same day as Reger's hurried departure and the U.S. Seventh Army's entering the outskirts of the city, a mob of German civilians broke into the Fuehrerbau, sweeping aside the military unit and embarking on an orgy of looting and destruction, as much a pointless too-late revolt against the Hitler régime as any desire for monetary gain. Cursing their Fuehrer mainly because he had led them to defeat, they broke open the doors of the vaults and seized any painting or other work of art they could lay their hands on. Some they destroyed, others they took away with them. They came back the next day and the days that followed. By the time American troops were able to restore order, 575 of the 723 items in the Fuehrerbau had been looted. All but twenty-two of the 262 paintings in the Schloss collection had vanished, though many of them were soon recovered.

On 1 May, in the midst of these turbulent events, Hans Reger had his forty-seventh birthday. He had little to celebrate.

For five years he had slaved in the Fuehrerbau, keeping his Linz records until the last few months in meticulous fashion, delighting in everything being neatly entered in its proper place. He had tried to flee to Alt Aussee, partly because there was no more reason for staying and partly to disprove the rumours that the Alt Aussee mine with all its priceless contents was to be blown up, an act of senseless destruction that affronted his sensibilities. He had failed to get there but, by leaving the Fuehrerbau, he had been spared watching a wild mob on the rampage, destroying his small orderly world of filing cabinets and rows of neatly stacked paintings, each carefully numbered.

*

Though Alt Aussee was by far the most important final hiding-place for Linz items, several small parts of the Linz collection were hidden elsewhere. The Hohenfurth monastery was used to store furniture and *objets d'art* belonging to the Mannheimer collection as well as a number of coin collections. At the Schloss Steiersberg, nearer Wiener-Neustadt, were stored various *objets d'art* as well as the collection of Count Lanckoronski looted from Poland in the autumn of 1939. Other parts of the Count's collection were hidden at Bad Aussee, where there were also various paintings and books, and at the Schloss Thuerntal. At the Schloss Kogl at St Georgen, Attergau were hidden cases of books sent by Dr Wolffhardt from Grundlsee. Even a small inn in the alpine village of St Agatha was utilized as a repository for paintings.

At the Schloss Weesenstein Hitler had stored a large number of prints and drawings, including the much-prized collection of the Amsterdam banker Franz Koenigs. These were seized by the Russians in June 1945, as were the paintings stored in the Dresden State Art Gallery after the Red Army entered the city.

The Schloss Thuerntal contained the major part of the collection of Baron Cassel. This had arrived at Alt Aussee in March 1944 in eighteen railway trucks, packed with crates and boxes marked with the code-name 'Berta', and escorted by men of the S.S. Given no notification whatsoever from France that it was on its way, Reimer was faced with the problem of finding the necessary storage space. He delegated the task to Dr Seiberl of the Viennese Institute for the Protection of Monuments, who had supervised the transporting of many art treasures from Vienna to Alt Aussee.

Going through the papers delivered with the consignment, Seiberl found that the entire collection had been confiscated from Baron Cassel and had come from Cannes and other storage places in the South of France. Because space at Alt Aussee was already at a premium, only the most valuable items were buried in the mine, the rest being moved on to the Schloss Thuerntal. The most important part of the collection was a group of late nineteenth-century French paintings, its total value estimated at being at least 1,500,000 reichsmarks.

The decision to move Germany's art treasures underground was not confined solely to Hitler's Linz collection. Orders were given to German museums to move their collections to subterranean depths out of range of Allied air attacks. At the Heilbronn salt-mine the Germans stored 830 paintings, 147 pieces of sculpture, 295 antiquities and 4,610 cases of books, the contents of museums at Karlsruhe, Mannheim, and Stuttgart, all of which had suffered heavily from bombing attacks. At the Kochendorf salt-mines the total was 534 paintings, 52 pieces of sculpture, 1,092 antiquities, and 3,600 cases of books from museums at Stuttgart, Cologne, and Heidelberg. At the Lauffen salt-mine near Bad Ischl, the city authorities of Vienna stored its art treasures. Besides numerous tapestries, a total of 1,408 paintings were hidden in the darkness of the mine, including works by Rembrandt, Titian, Breughel, and Duerer.

Many great works of art were unfortunately destroyed in Allied air attacks. The policy of utilizing the salt-mines was to make this total far less than it might have been. If Hitler had been indifferent to the fate of artistic masterpieces, as he was indifferent to the fate of the German people during the last months of the war, the story might have been very different. But he clung to his dreams of Linz to the very end, taking the trouble to issue orders to move works of art to places of safety. Fortunately he took this action in the spring of 1944. In his near-mad state after the attempt on his life on 20 July, he rapidly degenerated into a mood in which he was ready to pull down the whole of Europe with him into oblivion. If it had not been for his obsession with Linz, he might have ordered the burning of Europe's art treasures as he had burned books in the 1930s. But once the salt-mines policy was under way, he never attempted to reverse it.

The problems of the Allied commanders as their armies advanced across Europe towards Berlin were difficult and delicate. They were coming to Europe as liberators but they still needed to preserve the goodwill and co-operation of the occupied peoples in the difficult days that lay ahead after the cessation of hostilities. After years of being ground under the Nazi jackboot and enduring daily humiliations, the conquered peoples needed to reassert themselves as free nations, and their national pride meant everything to them. Part of that pride was their national treasures so brutally looted by the Nazis, and General Eisenhower and his subordinates were well aware of the need to get them returned as quickly as possible without hint of procrastination. Even before D-Day, orders had been given that this must be accomplished as swiftly as possible and without the incidents that might offend the bruised self-respect of the occupied peoples.

But where were the great art treasures hidden? Little information beyond the wildest of rumours had come out of Europe during the years of occupation. The problem now was to find them as quickly as was humanly possible.

CHAPTER TEN

Aladdin's Cave at Alt Aussee

The road to the salt-mine at Alt Aussee was a formidable obstacle for a lorry of any size, but once the salt-mine had been reached, it supplied the perfect hiding-place. The area was sparsely populated, the mine itself isolated, and the conditions underground almost constant throughout the year, the temperature varying only between 40° and 47° F. and the humidity remaining at about 65%. These were important considerations in the storing of old masters which would be easily damaged by adverse conditions. There was dampness at Alt Aussee but mostly in the tunnels and not in the chambers themselves. Only the suits of armour needed protecting with a heavy coating of grease to prevent oxidization.

It was the Viennese authorities who first realized what a perfect and absolutely safe repository Alt Aussee was and they took it over in 1942. Dismantled panels of the Millionen Zimmer and the Chinesisches Kabinett from Schoenbrunn were amongst the first art treasures sent there. As Allied bombing raids increased, forcing the Nazis to protect what was valuable to them, Hitler quickly appreciated that Alt Aussee was ideal for his own purpose. It found favour in his eyes because it was so near Berchtesgaden; he found comfort in knowing that his plunder of Europe's riches could be stored only a short car ride away. In 1943 he gave orders for commandeering Alt Aussee as the main repository for the Linz collection if the need arose. By 1944 it had arisen.

The mine at Alt Aussee consisted of a series of chambers, some of them extremely large, connected by a network of tunnels. Transportation was carried out by a miniature railway system which the Nazis gratefully took over, for walking the long distances between chambers through the low-ceilinged tunnels was extremely tiring.

The transformation of the mine was well organized. Great wooden tiers of shelves were built in the chambers, which were divided into numbered sections so that the location of any work of art could be recorded. As each work of art entered the mine it was also numbered and its description entered in one of a number of bulky ledgers. At first things went smoothly under the direction of Dr Reimer but the mine was badly understaffed for the crisis that was to come. In the last panic-stricken months of the war artistic treasures poured into this remote Austrian mountain village from the Fuehrerbau in Munich and a dozen other repositories, becoming a flood so great that the recording system broke down. Instead of having its own number, a painting would go underground bearing still the number of its consignment, or more than one number, or no number at all. The neatness in the chambers gave way to a higgledy-piggledy disorder as works of art were brought in and haphazardly stored in a corner. The chambers became a series of vast bric-à-brac shops but each without a proprietor who knew where everything was. In the semi-darkness it was difficult to realize the fabulous wealth represented by so much disorder.

As the countless lorries covered the winding road to Alt Aussee, unloading their cargo of art treasures before hurriedly departing, the number of works of art in the mine grew to astounding proportions. By far the biggest part was earmarked for Linz. Out of the ten thousand paintings finally stored in the mine, 6,755 belonged to Hitler, from which the collection for the designated Fuehrermuseum would be chosen. Of these 6,755, 5,350 were old masters whose total value, at today's prices, would be greater than the annual budget of many countries emerging in the world today. Besides the paintings, other Linz items in the salt-mine included 230 drawings and watercolours, 1,039 prints, 95 tapestries, 68 pieces of sculpture, 32 cases of coins and a numismatic library, 128 items of arms and armour, 79 baskets and 43 cases filled with *objets d'art*, 237 crates of books, and the Gordon Craig theatre archives, seized in France.

But this vast number of art treasures, specifically earmarked for Linz, formed only part of Hitler's possessions buried at Alt Aussee. The underground chambers also contained 209 paintings and 6 rugs intended for Hitler's castle at Posen; 534 paintings, 9 tapestries, 16 pieces of sculpture, 11 rugs, 7 portfolios of prints and 16 cases of *objets d'art* that were to form his personal collection at Berchtesgaden; and the 119 cases packed tight with the Fuehrer's books from his private Berlin library which had been moved to Alt Aussee because of the severe night-raids on the capital. Hitler also stored at the mine a number of reports, documents, and personal papers.

At Alt Aussee there were also a number of the world's greatest masterpieces which had become almost national shrines in the countries to which they belonged. Because of their importance Hitler deliberately made the question of their ownership ambiguous. He had seized them to protect them from Allied air attacks, but whether they would have been returned if the Nazis had won the war was, to say the least, problematical. They included the famous Ghent altarpiece of the 'Adoration of the Mystic Lamb', painted by Hubert and Jan van Eyck in 1432 and indisputably the greatest single work of art in Belgium. Despite being roughly handled and transported on the back of a lorry covered with a canvas sheet, it was still virtually undamaged. Also in the mine were the Dirk Bouts altarpiece from Louvain and Michelangelo's masterpiece, the marble Madonna from the Church of Notre Dame in Bruges, one of his earliest big works, sculptured by him in 1501 when he was twenty-six. In the same century it had been presented to the church where it had remained until September 1944, the Nazis carrying it off under the pretext that it must be saved from the Allied barbarians advancing on the city.

Hitler had permitted Goering, his greatest rival in art looting, to store some of his art treasures at Alt Aussee though overcrowding rigidly limited the numbers. But from his collection Goering was able to move to the mine 17 paintings, 11 cases of sculpture and bronzes, and a folio of drawings from the Naples Museum, originally kept by him in Berlin.

If the total number of works of art buried deep in the Alt Aussee salt-mine was staggering, their range was even more so. There was an ancient Greek sarcophagus, a masterpiece of sculpture looted from Salonika. There were paintings by Rembrandt and other great Dutch masters, canvases of various artists from the Rothschild, Gutmann, and Mannheimer collections, famous throughout Europe. There were the famous tempera panels of the fourteenth-century Hohenfurth altarpiece. There were pieces of sculpture that included Egyptian tomb figures, Roman portrait busts, Renaissance and Baroque bronzes, exquisite eighteenth-century French marbles and delicate Tanagra figures. There were tapestries from Cracow, furniture from the castle at Posen, rows of inlaid tables and cabinets from the Rothschild collection in Vienna, shelves and cases filled with porcelain, prints and drawings, some of which dated back to the sixteenth century. There was the celebrated Vermeer, 'Portrait of the Artist in his Studio', once owned by Count Czernin. There was the Naples Museum collection, including paintings by Titian, Raphael, Breughel, Lippi, Palma Vecchio, and Claude Lorrain that were sent to Monte Cassino for safety and looted en route to the Vatican. There were paintings looted from numerous private collections, including masterpieces by Rubens, Titian, Reynolds, Frans Hals, and others too numerous to mention. And there were also scores of inferior paintings by nineteenth-century German artists which Hitler still much admired, refusing to bow to expert opinion that most of them were so much rubbish.

It was from this vast accumulation of art treasures that the Linz museums were to be filled if the architectural plans could only be lifted from the drawing-board. But long before the Alt Aussee salt-mine was filled to its many roofs, that had become an impossibility, shattered with so many more of Hitler's dreams.

*

The Allied military authorities in Europe were well aware of the need for speed in restoring art treasures to their rightful owners. It was a heavy responsibility for there would be an outcry if they failed, for instance, to find the Ghent altarpiece which was a national shrine in Belgium. And the possibility could not be ruled out that some Nazis, as they went down to total defeat, would perpetrate a last-minute act of barbaric vandalism, a final gesture at the world which they were leaving.

As the Allied armies advanced, a great deal of information was obtained but it did not fit together to form a clear picture of the whereabouts of the bulk of the looted art treasures. And not one of the many jig-saw pieces bore the name of the Alt Aussee salt-mine.

The task of tracking down Nazi art plunder was given to a special section set up within the Supreme Headquarters, Allied Expeditionary Force. Named the Monuments, Fine Arts, and Archives Section, it was staffed by officers who in peacetime worked in museums or had wide knowledge of the art field. They acted as detectives, following up any clue that might lead to a hidden cache of art treasures, most often found in remote castles, villas, and monasteries. Urgency was needed not only to stop any last-minute destruction by the Nazis, but also to get there before the Russians, who were advancing rapidly from the East.

The M.F.A. & A. men set as their prime target the Ghent altarpiece. It was of supreme importance that it be found. They knew the Nazis had taken it away only the previous September and therefore the trail was still possibly warm enough to yield some clues. It was also so well known and revered that someone might know where it was hidden. And if it could be found, the M.F.A. & A. were convinced they would find a great deal more in the same place.

They made inquiries about the altarpiece. Soon they had collected information putting it in a dozen different places—the Rhine fortress of Ehrenbreitstein, the Berghof at Berchtesgaden, Goering's Karinhall estate, the vaults of the Berlin Reichsbank. Or it had been secretly flown to Spain, Switzerland, South America or any other neutral spot still left on the map. It was nothing but rumours, unbacked by a scrap of real evidence. The M.F.A. & A. men were baffled.

The break-through came from an art dealer in Luxembourg who told Captain Robert Posey, an M.F.A. & A. officer, that he had heard at some time that a salt-mine was being used. Where it was he did not know. It was just another unsupported rumour until at Trier Captain Posey interrogated a young German art scholar who had spent most of the war in France. His years were so tender and his appearance so unassuming that it was hard to believe his claim to have been in the confidence of Goering and other high Nazis in regard to their art collections. But nothing would shake him in his assertion that the Ghent altarpiece was hidden in a salt-mine in the remote Austrian village of Alt Aussee.

The masterpiece of the van Eycks had to be somewhere, if it hadn't been destroyed, and every other lead had failed. If it was at Alt Aussee, everything now depended on how fast the American Third Army could advance and so become the first troops to enter the isolated mountain region where the salt-mine lay. Maps were hastily consulted, the estimated distances the Russian and American armies were from Alt Aussee measured and re-measured. The margin was not great but the Russians might not make any haste if they did not know art treasures were hidden there because the area was of no strategic importance. It was the main hope of Captain Posey and his M.F.A. & A. colleagues as the German Army fell back before the advancing Third Army.

But others were also showing an interest in Alt Aussee. The region was commanded by Gauleiter Eigruber, who received early in April an ambiguous letter from Martin Bormann, conveying the Fuehrer's solemn instructions, two vital responsibilities that the Gauleiter must carry out to the last letter. He must ensure that the priceless treasures hidden in the Alt Aussee salt-mine did not, on any account, fall into the hands of the enemy. At the same time he must ensure that none of them suffered the slightest harm.

Eigruber cursed as he read these two impossible conditions. He must blow up the mine or let the enemy capture it, now that the Wehrmacht was no longer a coherent fighting force. He wasn't a magician, able to make thousands of paintings and pieces of sculpture and goodness knows what else vanish into thin air. He re-read the letter several times, trying vainly to puzzle out what was in the Fuehrer's mind, the main occupation of most leading Nazis during their last days of power in Europe. Did he or did he not, Eigruber asked himself, want the things blown up? It was the only thing to do if you didn't want the enemy to have them. Like most Nazis of his stamp, the Gauleiter was a man of action and little else. He now decided to act but prudently gave himself room to back-pedal quickly if he guessed wrong. After all, if he did nothing, the choice would soon be taken from him.

On 10 April the Inspector for the Upper Danube, a man named Glinz, arrived at the Alt Aussee salt-mine in a lorry carrying three large crates. Each was marked in black letters *'Marmor—Nicht Stuerzen'* ('Marble—do not drop'). But instead of marble, each crate contained a bomb weighing 100 lb. Glinz returned on 13 April and on 30 April with more cases until there were eight in all. He was to place them at strategic points along the tunnels, after showing documents that he was acting on the Gauleiter's instructions. If they went off, he estimated that the bombs would either destroy or badly damage the various chambers, and at the same time put out of action the pumping machinery controlling the water that was constantly seeping through. Thus any work of art not damaged by the explosions would be flooded and totally ruined. Glinz estimated that it would take weeks to dig through to any of the chambers.

Obedient to Eigruber's instructions, Glinz left the crates of bombs at the head of the mine, ready to take them underground with the greatest possible speed once the word was given. Still uncertain of the Fuehrer's reaction, Eigruber was ensuring that any explosion would be at the fifty-ninth minute of the eleventh hour.

On the afternoon of 30 April, a few hours after Glinz had delivered the last of his crated bombs, other visitors came to Alt Aussee, arriving in a small truck. There were three men—Dr Leopold Ruprecht, the man in charge of the Linz armour collection, Dr Schedelmann, an art dealer of Elisabethstrasse in Vienna, and Karl Kluge, their chauffeur.

Ruprecht, who was a morphine addict, produced papers signed by von Hummel, Bormann's personal secretary. Then, stating that he was acting on Bormann's verbal instructions, he asked for the box of gold coins recently transferred from the Hohenfurth monastery to Alt Aussee. The three men waited, Ruprecht barely able to contain his impatience, while the box was brought up from the mine after a considerable delay. It was about four feet long, weighing nearly a hundredweight. Inside were packed 2,200 gold coins, their total value a considerable fortune. Ruprecht signed a receipt, ordered the box to be placed on the truck and the three men drove away.

They drove to near-by Bad Aussee where they transferred themselves and the box of coins to a faster DKW saloon. Then they raced at high speed to Berchtesgaden, arriving there in the late evening. Kluge stood by as von Hummel came out to greet them. Ruprecht handed the box over to him and it was taken inside. The three men stayed the night and the next day Kluge drove Ruprecht and Schedelmann to their homes.

What happened to that vast number of gold coins can only be a matter of speculation. Eighteen years have passed and still no trace has been found of them or of Martin Bormann. It is possible they are buried deep in the Toplitzsee in the Styrian Alps where it is said that so much Nazi treasure is hidden, but because of their number and compactness, the coins would have been ideal for one man wishing to vanish from Germany and assume a different identity in another part of the world. He would need a great deal of money but not in so large a form as to arouse suspicions. He would have to vanish through many doors, each before it opened having its price which would have to be paid in an acceptable currency. And he would avoid banknotes like the plague when inflation could so easily make them worthless.

Martin Bormann's disappearance remains the outstanding mystery of the Nazi régime. Did he avoid the fate of his master in the Berlin bunker and achieve a total disappearance? Is he alive somewhere, accepted by other men, able to live without arousing speculation in other men's minds? If this is indeed the case, he may well owe his survival to a box of gold coins, seized for Linz, and stored in a Czech monastery until it finally found its way into one of the cold chambers in the Alt Aussee salt-mine.

And did others have the same idea as Bormann, not for reasons of personal survival, but because they wanted to keep the Nazi movement alive? In those last days many men turned to the Linz storehouses, seeking more practical uses for the contents than Hitler's dream of aggrandisement. One of them was Gerhardt Utikal, Rosenberg's second-in-command in Paris during the halcyon looting days. Though the Einsatzstab was defunct its administration lingered on, and in 1945 Utikal was head of its Berlin office. On the night of 26 April he arrived at the Schloss Neuschwanstein, said he was acting on orders and demanded that all the gold in store be handed over to him. He was given a small wooden box containing some gold coins of no great value.

The next day Utikal left, saying he would be delivering the coins to the Reich Treasurer, Herr Schwartz, in Munich, in accordance with his instructions. But he never went to Munich, going instead to the Einsatzstab's last headquarters—the Schloss Sandersdorf, situated about sixteen miles north-east of Ingolstadt in Bavaria. He stayed there for several days, informing the castle's owner, Count Basus, on leaving that he was going to Zell-am-See. But Utikal next turned up at the Schloss Kogl at St Georgen, Attergau, a Linz repository used by Wolffhardt for storing books. Again he demanded gold but was told there was none in the castle. He repeated his demands before being convinced and leaving empty-handed.

But wherever Utikal went, looking for gold, he always made the same statement. It was needed for 'the reconstruction of the party'.

*

Karl Sieber was a small man, almost insignificant in appearance. He was quiet and diffident, rarely pushed himself forward, preferring to go unnoticed rather than risk voicing an opinion, yet he was not without stature. He did not grovel, could not be easily intimidated, nor did not readily show fear. He was a self-contained man, having that unspoken dignity that clings to those who love and believe in the work they do, and wish no more than to be left alone to do it. It was Sieber, the first to be lost in a crowd, who perhaps did more than any other man to save the many art treasures buried in the Alt Aussee salt-mine from a senseless and barbaric destruction that would have impoverished mankind.

By trade Sieber was an art restorer. Before the war he worked in Berlin, occasionally selling a painting on the side to implement his income. He was a proficient and highly skilled craftsman, respected by some as an honest man in a corrupt age, and dismissed by others with contempt as a simpleton. He was entirely wrapped up in his work, so much so that he was not fully aware of the catastrophic changes taking place under his nose. If he wasn't interested in Hitler and National Socialism, it was because his mind was focused elsewhere.

In the early thirties Sieber was advised by a Jewish art dealer, for whom he did some work, to join the Nazi Party. The Jew could see that membership might be good for business but was still blind to the calamity that awaited his own race. Not greatly interested Sieber agreed, enrolled, and went back to restoring his beloved paintings.

He was a long way from being good fighting material but no man worked more willingly at his own craft. As the looted art treasures poured into Berlin from all parts of Europe, he never lacked work to do, particularly in the case of canvases damaged en route. In 1943 his life was uprooted when he was suddenly sent to Alt Aussee as the official restorer soon after the Nazis had commandeered the mine from the Austrians. When the Ghent altarpiece arrived at the mine in September 1944 the large panel depicting St John had split lengthwise with the grain of the wood. For many hours Sieber worked on it, patiently carrying out an 'invisible repair'. He worked for long hours underground, living like a mole, but grateful that not even the upheavals of war had separated him from great masterpieces of art.

At the mine Sieber wore a uniform that was too large and made him appear slightly ridiculous. It consisted of baggy white trousers, a white jacket with a wide collar and bearing two rows of large black buttons on its front with several more running from cuff to elbow on the sleeves, a tape drawstring tied round his middle, and a plain black cap. White was chosen because it was easier to see against the blackness underground but the overall effect was to make Sieber look like one of Walt Disney's seven dwarfs.

The local miners, who had once worked the salt, were also small men like Sieber. They liked him because he was quiet and reserved, and a welcome change from his fellow-Germans, most of whom were arrogant bullies who looked upon Austria as no different from any other occupied country. Sieber kept to himself, dividing his days between the mine and the near-by house where he lived with his wife and small daughter.

Late in April 1945 local members of the Austrian resistance movement decided that they had sufficient grounds for believing that the Nazis were preparing to blow up the Alt Aussee mine. The three visits by Inspector Glinz had not gone unnoticed, particularly as he did not usually soil his hands by hawking around cases of marble. The war was in its final stages so that if anything was to happen, it would happen soon. But the main obstacles to any preventive action were the S.S. men still guarding the mine.

The resistance men ruled out a pitched battle. They could easily be held off long enough for the Germans to detonate any laid explosives. The only alternative was to enter the mine without arousing suspicion, but they could think of no way of achieving this. Eventually they settled on a desperate gamble. They decided to contact the quiet little man who was so unlike the other Germans, enlist his aid and pray that he did not report them to his Nazi superiors.

They made contact with Sieber at his house. If they had known him better, they would have been aware that there was no gamble. When they told him what they suspected, Sieber's dominant reaction was horror that so much glorious proof of man's aspirations over the centuries to create great beauty might be wantonly destroyed. He was little interested in who controlled the Alt Aussee mine, only that no harm should befall a single painting, not even those by Hitler's favourite nineteenth-century German painters whose work Sieber little admired. He agreed at once to help them. To do otherwise would have been a negation of his whole life.

Ignoring the fact that he was risking death, Sieber discussed several plans with them, all of which were rejected. Finally they hit upon one that was daring and yet feasible. Get into the mine and blow it up first, but with meticulous care so that the Nazis would be cut off from the chambers and would be unable to blow them up themselves. With the Allied armies advancing so fast, they calculated that a week's delay would be sufficient.

Having worked in the mine for two years, Sieber knew every yard of the network of tunnels. He drew a detailed plan, showing where each one of the mine's chambers was situated—the Kaiser Josef where was stored the great marble Madonna of Michelangelo, standing out amidst a host of artistic treasures; the Mineral Kabinett where the dominant item was the Ghent altarpiece; the Springerwerke, containing more than two thousand paintings, crammed on double wooden tiers round three walls and down the centre; the Kapelle, housing the armour from Spain which had once formed the magnificent Konopischt collection of the Archduke Ferdinand; the chamber where the Austrian miners had built an altar in memory of their country's dead hero, Dr Dollfuss; and the Kammergrafen, the largest chamber of all and the most remote, with several galleries on different levels, each packed high from floor to ceiling with paintings, sculpture, tapestries, rugs, rare books, and furniture.

Well aware that the Kammergrafen was the safest from accidental flooding or the collapsing of roofs, Hitler had ordered that it be used only for the Linz items. Nothing entered the chamber unless Hitler had already indicated that it was worthy to go into the museums he was planning to build in his own memory.

Besides plotting the various chambers, Sieber also drew the network of tunnels through which a miniature train ran on a narrow gauge, drawn by a small petrol engine and pulling coaches that were open wooden boxes about five feet long and two feet wide, large enough for two men—who learned quickly to keep their heads down—to travel in. Sometimes the tunnels were wide, with plenty of clearance above and on both sides of the trains, but there were also places where the roof was low and the coaches scraped against jagged rocks. At points along the tunnels Sieber marked the heavy iron doors that led to the chambers.

The Austrians examined his plan carefully. Spots were marked where small charges of dynamite could be exploded, capable of bringing down the tunnels, thus effectively barring the way to the chambers, but not damaging them. There was only one man who could enter the mine without suspicion and carry out the operation—Sieber himself. He was supplied with the dynamite, fuses, and detonators and told in detail exactly what he must do. He performed the task perfectly, bringing down layers of rock but not blasting through to the chambers themselves. He was not caught or even suspected of being a saboteur. For too long he had been dismissed as a harmless type who did his job well, but was incapable of hurting a fly.

News of the damage to the mine was sent to Gauleiter Eigruber, still tortured with indecision, trying to decide whether to blow up the Alt Aussee mine or not, tempted to end the war and his own years of power with one enormous explosion. He was so enraged by this act of sabotage that he ordered the rounding up of every possible suspect so that they might be shot without the nicety of inquiring if they were guilty or not.

But Eigruber had left it too late for even this last act of revenge. The U.S. Third Army had been pushing hard for Alt Aussee, its troops alerted as to its importance even though few of them had ever heard of it. Tactical units were ordered to advance at breakneck speed, although it meant diverting them from the main task of finally defeating the disintegrating German Army. They raced through Bad Ischl, barely pausing to take prisoner the increasing number of Germans who came out with their arms aloft, anxious to surrender. In the village of Alt Aussee they came up against their last obstacle, the S.S. troops who had grown soft during the years of idleness, bored with guarding their Fuehrer's loot that had been gathered from a dozen different countries. They saw the determined American troops and wisely deciding that discretion was the better part of valour, put up their hands also. From the village it was barely a mile to the salt-mine that had become Hitler's treasure chest.

The first troops to reach the mine were men of the 80th Infantry Division. They placed a heavy guard around it and waited for the M.F.A. & A. men to arrive. The first to come was Captain Posey, accompanied by Private Lincoln Kirstein, who invariably worked with him. Armed with acetylene lamps as torches, the two men entered the damp passageway and stumbled a quarter of a mile before they were stopped by a fall of debris, the work of Karl Sieber. It looked as if it would take weeks to clear away the rocks blocking the tunnel but American troops, aided by some of the Austrian miners, worked feverishly and managed to clear a path through the fall within twenty-four hours. Posey and Kirstein scrambled over the rocks, managed to open the ugly iron door and entered the first chamber. Acetylene lamps held high, they gazed in wonderment at the scene that greeted them. As far as they could see there were art treasures, piled haphazardly, looking neglected, this one large room containing more wealth than existed in many museums. It was the first inkling of the fantastic discoveries that lay ahead as the tunnels were cleared and the other chambers entered, each yielding further tremendous wealth, and making the Allies realize that the extent of Hitler's looting was in reality far greater than even their wildest speculations.

By then they had found the ledgers that contained the record of the art treasures delivered to Alt Aussee. Though the last entries were chaotic, they revealed enough to show that Alt Aussee was the chief treasure store. There was the Ghent altarpiece, Michelangelo's Madonna from Bruges, great masterpieces from the museums and private collections of Europe. Other M.F.A. & A. men arrived, wandering from one dim chamber to the next, and for all it was an overwhelming and unbelievable experience.

But there was little time to gape open-mouthed. Now started

the tremendous task of bringing each work of art up to the sunlight after it had been buried for months in the semi-darkness, of sorting them, discovering their rightful owners, and making sure they were safely returned. As they were later to claim about the concentration camps, the German people were unaware that the treasure-chambers of the Alt Aussee mine existed. But unlike Dachau, Auschwitz and Buchenwald, here proper restitution could be made to the victims of Nazi barbarism.

*

The paintings were given priority because they were so easily movable. The most valuable came up first under the direction of the M.F.A. & A. men. Wearing thick sweaters to enable them to work for several hours in the cold, they examined hundreds of canvases, framed and unframed, deciding their quality in snap judgements because time was important. Invariably they selected any painting bearing the stencil 'E.R.R.'—Einsatzstab Reichsleiter Rosenberg—on the assumption that any painting which had formed part of the great Jewish collections was sure to be valuable. In one afternoon they would select and bring to the surface as many as two hundred canvases, ready for transport to the clearing-house at Munich. The big canvases were an easy choice—the Titians, Van Dycks, Rembrandts and Breughels. Otherwise they worked on the principle that if they reacted in those dim chambers, on top their decision was usually justified. Restored to daylight, a painting would immediately glow with an intense beauty, as if it was also celebrating the sudden end of its gloomy captivity.

Manual help was supplied by troops and the local miners— small men living in the surrounding villages whose ancestors had toiled for five centuries in the Alt Aussee salt-mine. They were cheerful, hard-working, and thankful the Nazis had gone. They would hold up each canvas for inspection, place protective pads on it if it was selected, and then load it on the small train for the start of the journey out of the mine. The pads were made out of felt and a roll of lace curtaining found in the mine.

Slowly the M.F.A. & A. men worked their way through the various chambers, bringing some semblance of order where chaos had existed, working feverishly to keep from freezing as much as because they wanted to get the job finished. On the surface convoys of trucks had been organized in a shuttle-service to Munich, the mine's entrance being wide enough for them to be loaded two at a time. As each canvas came out of the mine, its number and other details were carefully recorded, one copy going with the convoy and another staying at the mine. So that the evacuation of the mine could be completed as quickly as possible, selection and transportation went on for twelve hours a day by means of two shifts underground.

Each truck was loaded with about 150 canvases plus a few odd pieces of sculpture or *objets d'art*. Six trucks formed a convoy and the three convoys were driven by eighteen U.S. Army Negro drivers, each of them a highly skilled artist behind the wheel, but with a happy-go-lucky disposition that refused to be over-awed by the historic and monetary value of their precious cargoes as they sped down the precipitous road to Alt Aussee village, the first of many steep mountain gradients. As Hans Reger had once sweated, the M.F.A. & A. men never completely relaxed until they heard the last convoy had safely reached Munich, at last banishing from their minds visions of over-turned trucks, surrounded by piles of centuries-old masterpieces smashed beyond repair, and the terrible repercussions that would then ensue.

On leaving the mine each loaded convoy was escorted by a jeep. At Bad Aussee two armoured vehicles from the 11th Armoured Division took over, acting as front and rear guard. Because a truck breaking-down could result in a serious delay, they were all only three-quarters filled so that the five could take aboard the cargo of the sixth if it fell by the wayside. In case of any delay, both armoured vehicles were equipped with radio to summon help, a necessary precaution as small bands of S.S. troops were still roaming the mountains, mostly bent on wilful destruction, unable to accept total defeat after the past's glorious victories.

After passing through the narrow main street of Bad Aussee,

the trucks rolled through a small valley before climbing upwards towards the Poetschen Pass. Then the nerve-racking
descent by way of sharp hairpin bends until St Agatha was
reached. Onwards through Goisern, Lauffen and Bad Ischl before reaching the picturesque town of St Gilgen, skirting past
Alpine lakes, through densely wooded hills to Salzburg and the
final long road to Munich. As the line of drab-looking trucks
sped onwards, the people sometimes came out to watch, little
guessing the vast wealth concealed by the black tarpaulins.

In Munich the trucks were quickly unloaded before the return journey to Alt Aussee. The canvases were rapidly examined, records investigated to find out who had owned them and
then they were sent on. Besides carrying out the policy of speedy
restitution, the Allies were anxious to end as fast as possible their
own responsibility for any priceless painting that came into
their custody. But as there were thousands of paintings, it was
inevitable that the time taken dragged into weeks until the last
painting was delivered to Munich and at Alt Aussee could begin
the more difficult task of bringing out the pieces of sculpture,
the crates of books, and the antique furniture.

Underground the mine's chambers were gradually being
emptied, but as space was cleared, allowing the farthest recesses
to be explored, new discoveries were made. None was greater
than the two inconspicuous-looking cartons found in the corner
of one of the galleries of the Kammergrafen, hidden by some
Renaissance bronzes. They were not labelled, being about two
feet square and feeling surprisingly light when lifted. At first
antique glassware was suspected so the lids were carefully prised
open to avoid breakages, but inside were seen only a number of
plain cardboard boxes. One was carefully opened to reveal a
glittering golden pendant, studded with emeralds, rubies, and
pearls that were breathtakingly beautiful. Between them the two
cartons held forty cardboard boxes, containing exquisite neck-
laces, pendants, brooches and rings. These were the famous
Rothschild jewels, worth a king's ransom. Wisely it was decided
not to risk loading them on a truck. Early next morning the two
cartons, which any thief would have given his soul to possess,
were taken to Munich by an unobtrusive U.S. Army jeep.

The two biggest problems facing the M.F.A. & A. men were still in the Alt Aussee mine—the Ghent altarpiece and the marble Madonna of Michelangelo. Because of the national storm that would rage if anything went wrong, extra precautions were taken. Two trucks were earmarked for the job and specially overhauled to reduce the risk of a breakdown. Their two Negro drivers were impressed with the importance of their cargoes and for once they acted as if they were impressed.

The Madonna was brought out first, wrapped so heavily that it was a shapeless bundle. Twelve of the little Austrian miners lifted it from the train and carried it to the waiting truck, sliding it between the two cases that contained the coin collection Adolf Hitler had dreamed of giving to his Linz museums. Blankets were stuffed between the cases and the statue so that the Madonna was jammed tight. To make sure she would not slide, a large case containing the Greek sarcophagus from Salonika was finally placed aboard and secured to the floor. Then up came the ten cases containing the Ghent altarpiece and they were placed on the other truck in parallel rows and lashed upright. Other cases were pushed in between to jam them tight and the next day the two trucks started on the journey to Munich, going slowly down the steep road to the village. Behind them were left the men still working at the mine, breathing sighs of relief.

Slowly the chambers thinned out until one by one they became empty. The last crate of books was brought up, the last piece of sculpture, the very last object. It had taken many weeks but at last Hitler's buried treasure was back in the open to be enjoyed by men once more instead of being hidden deep in the ground. The last convoy started the journey from the Alt Aussee mine to Munich.

Elsewhere the probing was going on, the determination to find out how Hitler had accumulated his vast amount of loot and who had helped him. As the convoys of trucks from the mine drove through Bad Aussee, they passed a large villa known to the Allied authorities as 'House 71'. Inside it men of the Art Looting Investigation Unit of the Office of Strategic Services carried out daily interrogations that lasted for hour after hour, slowly piecing together scraps of information until a picture was formed. Then they began to understand the methodical ruthlessness employed by Hitler and other Nazi leaders to plunder like common thieves the greatest of man's creations over the centuries of European civilization.

CHAPTER ELEVEN

The Allies Make Restitution

It was like a film being run backwards, everything repeated in reverse. During the years of Nazi conquest the looted art treasures had poured into Munich to be numbered and catalogued before being hidden away. Now they were pouring back as the M.F.A. & A. men rooted out the Nazi storehouses, searching castles, farms, out-of-the-way villas, and certainly every salt-mine. In the Munich area alone more than 175 caches of Nazi loot were discovered and emptied. Every recovered art treasure was sent to the Central Collecting Point, set up by the Allied authorities inside the former Verwaltungsbau ('Party building') that formed a pair with the Fuehrerbau in the Koenigsplatz. Here art experts came from France, Belgium, Holland, and the other occupied countries to help identify both the works of art and their owners. Each man in the Verwaltungsbau worked tirelessly, caught up in the emotional exhilaration of righting a great wrong. By October 1945 more than 13,000 works of art had passed through the building.

In many instances restitution was swift and efficient, particularly if a great masterpiece was involved. Once it had been discovered, its owner was known beyond all doubt. But discovery was not always quick, small caches of looted art treasures not being found until some time after the war ended, and then usually stumbled upon in some remote spot. And there were also the little-known works of art and those not readily identifiable; if German records did not exist, it often took many months to ascertain who the owners were. But despite the many frustrations and delays, the work proceeded steadily, though often slowly. The restoration of Nazi loot accumulated over seven years could not be achieved in the same number of months, and it is significant that the Americans were not ready to hand over the Central Collecting Point to the Germans until as late as 1951.

If thousands of works of art were safely restored to their rightful owners, how many thousands are still missing? Even nearly twenty years later it is still difficult to give a reliable estimate. The Italians have said they have 600 great paintings still missing but they were looted only towards the end of the war. No official survey has yet been attempted to cover the whole of Europe. Yet because great works of art so often arouse man's greed and insatiable desire for possession, the Nazi wartime loot still to come to light must be extremely large. Much was no doubt destroyed in the mass air-raids on German cities but many more art treasures must still be hoarded by private collectors, who are unable to part with them. The situation is further complicated in the case of the Jewish collections whose owners later died, so that no one now knows how much was seized in the first place. Without doubt the two largest looters were Hitler and Goering, and records exist as to what they accumulated, but fewer details are known of the many smaller fry who dabbled with greedy fingers. They had no organization or network of agents, only their personal avarice and eye for an opportunity. It must be a conservative estimate to state that at least 100,000 works of art were looted by the Nazis during their years of power in Europe.

*

In their search for Nazi plunder, beyond all question the two largest hauls of the M.F.A. & A. men were found at Alt Aussee and Schloss Neuschwanstein, the Einsatzstab Rosenberg repository. Between them they contained well over 30,000 art treasures and though doubtless many would not have been considered worthy for Linz when the promised post-war sorting-out took place, nevertheless they were held in Hitler's name and were his for the asking.

The Rosenberg confiscations, the result of organized looting on a scale rarely equalled, deserve closer examination. At Neuschwanstein there were 21,903 works of art. Out of the 200 collections represented, the Rothschilds headed the list with 3,978 of their looted art treasures stored in the castle and many others elsewhere. Next came the Kahn collection with 1,202 works of art, David-Weill with 1,121, Lévy de Benzion with 989, and André and Jacques Seligmann with 556.

Out of the 21,903 art treasures, 10,890 were paintings, some of them amongst the most valuable in the world. They included 4,525 engravings, 3,027 oil paintings, 1,332 drawings, 766 water-colours, 442 miniatures, and thirteen reproductions. There were 2,477 items of furniture, which included 277 chandeliers and 979 chairs and sofas, most of them extremely valuable antiques. Pieces of sculpture totalled 583, including 129 in bronze or other metals, 110 in marble, sixty-five in wood, and seventy-four in terracotta, porcelain, or clay. There were 583 items classified as textiles, including sixty-six Gobelins tapestries and 291 carpets. Handmade objects numbered 5,825, including 252 ceramics, 243 pieces of jewellery, 844 rare coins, 335 pieces of porcelain, and seventy-four objects that contained rare gems. There were 259 antiquities from such places as China, Ancient Greece, Asia Minor, and Egypt. And, finally, there were 1,286 assorted items, amongst them 183 woodcarvings, sixty-eight works of Japanese art, 583 of porcelain and stoneware, and ninety-two of semi-precious gems and ivories.

At today's values, their total worth can only be described as astronomical, sufficient to buy a number of Polaris submarines. Rarely in history has so much artistic wealth been collected under one roof and to such an extent that the castle could offer shelter to only a few of the many people it normally housed. Once the New Europe had been established, the lesser Nazis would have impatiently waited for Hitler to take what he wanted, leaving the rest to be shared out amongst them as their fruits of victory.

*

The investigation into the Sonderauftrag Linz, ordered by the Allies as soon as Germany had surrendered, had three main purposes. It aimed at discovering the personalities involved and the particular part each of them played; classifying the methods employed in amassing the collections; and ascertaining the sources from which the various works of art were obtained. The investigation itself was a tacit admission that it was Hitler who was the greatest of the art looters and not Goering, as had been widely believed before the Allied art experts had entered Germany.

Interrogation of some of the principals involved was carried out at length and in great detail. Hermann Voss, described by his questioners as a 'sour-puss', was interrogated at Alt Aussee from 15 August to 15 September, and for a further five days at Nuremberg in the following November. Karl Haberstock was questioned for thirty-six days at Alt Aussee, starting on 20 August. Heinrich Hoffmann was questioned for twenty-one days, starting on 8 June, and again at Nuremberg in the following November. Others brought to Alt Aussee for interrogation were Kajetan Muehlmann, Walter Hofer, Bruno Lohse, Ernst Buchner, Walter Bornheim the Munich art dealer, and Frauelein Gisela Limberger, confidential secretary to Goering.

Other interrogations were carried out elsewhere. Frau Maria Dietrich was questioned at Velden in Bavaria on 18 August and several times again at Munich in the October and November. Hans Reger was interrogated for ten days at Munich from 1 November. Hildebrandt Gurlitt, still homeless after being bombed-out in Dresden, was seen at the Aschbach estate, where he was living with his family, on 3 October. Leopold Ruprecht was interrogated about the Linz armour collection at Zell-am-See on 1 September and Adolf Weinmueller, owner of auction-houses in Vienna and Munich, was seen on 10 November at Tegernsee in Bavaria. Wolffhardt could not be questioned as he was reported missing on the Russian front. There were also three other men not available who could have told more about Linz than anyone else. Hans Posse and Adolf Hitler were dead, and Martin Bormann had wisely decided it was time to vanish.

Though these interrogations were exhaustive, none of the members of the Linz organization were prosecuted for war crimes.

In addition to these interrogations officers of the Art Looting Investigation Unit, set up within the Office of Strategic Services by the American Government, were able to unearth and examine a large number of valuable documents. Perhaps the most valuable—the official card catalogue of the collections for the Fuehrermuseum—was beyond their reach, being stored at the Schloss Weesenstein, near Dresden, which was captured by the Red Army. Though applications were made, the Russians refused to release it, being ill-disposed to give away anything during those post-war days of suspicion.

But there was plenty of other valuable material. The O.S.S. men were able to examine all Reger's records and photographic files, kept at the Fuehrerbau and miraculously undamaged by the rioting mobs in the previous April. At Alt Aussee they found the records of the paintings received at the mine, contained in thirty-one volumes, numbered with green figures. Also at the mine they found a rich harvest stored underground: various reports received by Bormann from Dr Posse; a card catalogue of the Linz armour collection in two wooden boxes; a card catalogue of the Linz library in eighteen drawers plus other records contained in four large ledgers; a catalogue of the Rothschild and other confiscated Jewish collections; a portfolio of works purchased by the Dienststelle Muehlmann; and an inventory of some of the items obtained from the Einsatzstab Rosenberg.

Other important finds were made at Berchtesgaden. In Hitler's private library were albums, bound in dark brown leather, each containing about fifty photographs of art treasures bought for Linz. On each cover was stamped in gold the title 'Gemälde-galerie Linz'. Several of the volumes were missing and all were numbered, the highest being thirty-one. Also in Hitler's library were other albums, this time grey with black spines, and containing photographs of Linz items that had come from the Rothschild collection in Vienna and other Viennese Jewish collections. One other discovery at Berchtesgaden was a bound typewritten list of the art treasures 'safeguarded' in France, listed in alphabetical order.

In their search for evidence the O.S.S. men were able to examine Maria Dietrich's ledgers and receipted bills, held at Velden and Munich; documents, letters, and photographs belonging to Karl Haberstock (who died soon after the war) as well as thirty files of his correspondence, dated 1940–42, all with him at Aschbach where he was still taking refuge; letters between Bormann and Hans Posse, found filed in the Berlin Reich Chancellery; thirty-nine volumes, bound in brown leather, containing photographs of works of art seized by the Einsatzstab Rosenberg and presented to Hitler on his birthday on 20 April, 1943, found at the Schloss Neuschwanstein; a catalogue of the Mannheimer collection, prepared by Muehlmann, and found lodged in a Dutch bank; and catalogues, correspondence, and accounts of the Linz coin collection, maintained at the Kunsthistorisches Institut in Vienna.

Out of this material and much else, reports on the Sonderauftrag Linz, the Goering collection, and the Einsatzstab Rosenberg were produced by officers of the Art Looting Investigation Office. The officers, all Americans, were James Plaut, Theodore Rousseau (now Curator of Paintings at the Metropolitan Museum, New York), and S. Lane Faison, jnr. (now Chairman of the Art Department, Williams College, Williamstown, Massachusetts). Their reports were classified as 'controversial' and submitted to the judicial authorities at Nuremberg. Later they were sent to Washington as the property of the Department of State.

*

In the summer of 1941 Adolf Hitler came desperately near to winning the war and creating his New Order in Europe.

Though he had been obsessed by his dream of Linz since 1938, by the order of things it could not take priority while hostilities still raged. Linz was to be created out of victory, and victory could only be achieved by reducing the hostility of the occupied peoples to a minimum. He needed every German unit on the Russian front and already resistance movements were tying down too many of his soldiers in the West. To avoid creating further antagonism, Hitler was prepared to build up his Linz collections from the art treasures of the occupied countries only if these transactions could be clothed with the appearance of legality, if not with legality itself.

He schooled himself to be patient. He ordered that all bills presented to the Sonderauftrag Linz should be promptly and fully paid. He avoided plundering the public collections, though he exercised no such restraint in Eastern Europe. He seized Jewish and enemy property but still took the trouble to promulgate special Nazi laws that would lend authority to his actions. He exercised this deliberate self-restraint, yet still amassed the greatest personal art collection the world has known.

If Hitler had won the war, would he have remained squeamish? Would he have carried on with the kid-glove methods? The answers can only be speculation, but, on the evidence, it is unlikely. Once the war was over and the New Order established, his psychological need to create his vision of Linz would have come to the forefront. He would probably have plundered the Louvre as ruthlessly as he had plundered the great Jewish collections. Linz would be the ugly duckling changed into a swan, a drab industrial town transformed into the glittering peak of European culture, unequalled by any of the great capitals. It would not only be Prague that would have been in danger of becoming no more than a German village.

For Hitler, the Linz dream held two potent attractions that never faded. It would glorify his memory as the genius who had remade Europe single-handed, and it would satisfy his desire for dramatic transformations. Making Berlin or Munich greater held little appeal. But taking his home-town, where he was still remembered as a boy, and waving his wand over it like a fairy godmother—that satisfied his need to express his power in a melodramatic fashion which all men could witness and marvel at.

Hitler planned the looting of art treasures as a department of State, placing the Sonderauftrag Linz in the highest category of Nazi looting enterprises. He also exercised over it a greater degree of personal control than over any other organization not directly concerned with waging the war. The Sonderauftrag was his 'special baby', created for a purpose closer to his heart than almost any other. In war looting is inevitable and usually blindly rapacious. Hitler showed it could be efficiently and expertly carried out, and aligned to a central purpose. He held back only until the last enemy was defeated.

His programme of plunder went deeper than surface events and wasn't confined to switching around the works of art so that there was a conglomeration in a town called Linz while others were stripped bare. He sought also to change the course of Art, making men see it as he wanted them to see it. He wanted to pervert artistic taste to his own ends.

In a Reich totally committed to conquering Europe the leading Nazis had little time for culture. Men were fighting machines and women bred fat babies. But once the war was over, other hungers would arise. Linz would be Hitler's proof that the Nazis could be as cultural as the next man, as long as it was within the dictates of their own philosophy. Thus the old masters would be accepted but only a few non-German painters born after the beginning of the nineteenth century would be accorded any value, the rest thrust into oblivion.

This was Hitler's theory of Art, as it would survive in the New Europe. Any artist, whose personal vision of the world was condemned by the Fuehrer, would be condemned by other men also. Thus Art itself would be debased until honest men looked upon it with contempt. It is arguable whether in time the looting itself would prove the greater crime against mankind.

*

Hitler's dream of conquest failed, his vision of Linz was stillborn. Today the town is largely as it was on that March evening when Hitler came in his Mercedes-Benz and aroused the people to a frenzied delirium. No one has yet succeeded in moving the railway station or rebuilding the bridge across the Danube, joining the town to the populous suburb of Urfahr. The Franz Josef Platz is still as it was and though the population has risen by fifty per cent, this has been due to the natural growth of industries such as iron and steel, textiles and chemicals. The town's most infamous son had nothing to do with it.

What is missing from Linz is the shadow of the cultural greatness that Adolf Hitler threatened to thrust upon it. The loss is not regretted. The people of Linz prefer things as they are because it is the world they know and accept. One can only hope that if a second Hitler came to the town, riding in an equally imposing chariot and supported by as many loud-mouthed fanatics, the people would accord him a quite different reception.

Index

INDEX

INDEX

Nationalism, 8

Nattier, Jean Marc, 29

Nazi Party (German National Socialists), Naziism and Nazis, 2, 16, 18, 22, 23, 45, 48, 53, 57, 68, 84, 86, 98–113 *passim*, 124, 125, 131, 137, 168; led by gangsters, 61–2; and Mannheimer, 79; and Linz agents, 88; and works of art, 113, 116; and Sieber, 163; in war and peace, 180

Negro drivers, 169, 171

Netherlands, The, *see* Holland

Neue Berg, 31, 149

'Neue Linzer Bibliothek', 117–24

Neufforge, Baron and Baroness, 120, 121

Neufforge book collection (Berne), 120, 121

Neumann, Josef, 6

Neurath, Reichsprotektor Baron von, 40

Neuschwanstein railway station, 61, 64

Neuschwanstein, Schloss, *see* Schloss Neuschwanstein

'New Order in Europe', Hitler's, 178, 179

Nice, 100, 137, 139

Nicolas, Etienne, 85, 98, 100

Niedermeyer, Ferdinand, 82–3

Notre Dame, Church of (Bruges), 156

Nuremberg, 49, 51; Nazi rallies at, 7

Nuremberg trials, 60; and investigations, 176

O.K.W. (Oberkommando der Wehrmacht: German High Command), 39

Obersalzberg, 16, 20, 74

Oertel, Dr Rudolf, 25, 128

Oesterreichische Galerie (Vienna), 28, 33

Opočno Castle (Czechoslovakia), 38

Paintings looted and missing, 112

Palaces, Russian, looted, 115

Palais Rothschild (Vienna), 30

Palamedes (painter), 76

Palma Vecchio, 99, 157

Pannini, Giovanni Paolo, 91, 95, 108, 110

Paris, 23, 52, 53, 55–67, 69, 70, 78, 83–96 *passim*, 128–33 *passim*, 137–41 *passim*

Paris Commune (1873), 57

Parmigianino, Francesco (Mazzola), 76, 108

Pellepoix, Darquier de, 139, 141, 142

Perdoux, Yves, 94

Perugia collection, 112

Picasso, Pablo, 93

Pissarro, Camille, 96

Pitti Gallery (Florence), 109, 111

Place du Marché St. Honoré, 99

Plague in Florence, The (Makart), 21, 109–10

Poellnitz, Baron von, 86, 100, 103, 132

Poland, 16, 47–52, 68, 82

Pollaiuolo, Antonio, 112

Polyhymnia (Muse of song and poetry), statue by Canova, 34

Pompadour, Madame de, 26, 95; her portrait by Boucher, 28, 64

Portrait of an Artist in his Studio (Vermeer), 34–6, 157

Posen, 156, 157

Posey, Captain Robert, 159, 167

Posse, Dr Hans (Director of Dresden Art Gallery), 18–20, 21–7 *passim*, 31, 40, 42–3, 93, 99, 100, 117, 119, 125, 128, 129, 135–7, 177, 178; his first report on Vienna loot, 27; second ditto, 29, 30; further reports, 32, 177; and Ganymede; 33; and 'Czernin Vermeer', 35–6, in Poland, 49–52; and Goering, 54, 58, 60, 64–6, 67, 69, 74–5; and Holland, 68–77 *passim*; Adviser on Special Questions, 69; his interview with Hitler, 72; and Baldung's Venus, 74–5; and Mannheimer collection, 81; his travelling facilities, 86; his funds, 87; and Hoffmann, 88, 89; and Goepel, 91; and Maria Dietrich,

INDEX